Twayne's United States Authors Series

EDITOR OF THIS VOLUME

Warren French

Indiana University

Carson McCullers

TUSAS 354

CARSON McCULLERS

By MARGARET B. McDOWELL

University of Iowa

TWAYNE PUBLISHERS

A DIVISION OF G. K. HALL & CO., BOSTON

Published in 1980 by Twayne Publishers,
A Division of G. K. Hall & Co.
All Rights Reserved

Printed on permanent/durable acid-free paper and bound
in the United States of America

First Printing

Frontispiece photo of Carson McCullers, August 1943.
Photograph by Paul Stewart.
Courtesy of *Ledger-Enquirer*, Columbus, Georgia.

Library of Congress Cataloging in Publication Data

McDowell, Margaret B
Carsons McCullers.

(Twayne's United States authors series ; TUSAS 354)
Bibliography: p. 152 - 56
Includes index.
1.   McCullers, Carson Smith, 1917 - 1967—Criticism
and interpretation.
I.   Title.
PS3525.A1772Z76   813'.5'2   79-13361
ISBN 0-8057-7297-9

Contents

About the Author

Margaret B. McDowell is Professor of Rhetoric at the University of Iowa, where she has been a member of the faculty since 1967 and was vice-chair of the Faculty Senate in 1975 - 76. She is a teacher in the Women's Studies Program and served as first chairperson of the program. She has been a member of the executive committees of the Women's Caucus for the Modern Languages and of the Midwest Modern Language Association. A summa cum laude graduate of Coe College, she received the M.A. in creative writing and the Ph.D. in English from the University of Iowa. She formerly taught at Kansas State University, Pittsburg, and at MacMurray College, Jacksonville, Illinois.

Professor McDowell is the author of *Edith Wharton* in the Twayne United States Authors Series. She has written essays on Wharton's use of the supernatural, her short story techniques, and the feminist values in her fiction. Her other writing includes articles on the rhetoric of contemporary feminism, the teaching of language arts to children, children's literature, college composition, Southern women writers, and Afro-American women writers.

Preface

For over thirty-five years critics have written continually on the work of Carson McCullers. Four books on her life and work have appeared: *The Ballad of Carson McCullers* by Oliver Evans, written in 1966, before her death, and three volumes thereafter, simply entitled *Carson McCullers*—one by Dale Edmonds and one by Lawrence Graver in 1969 and another by Richard M. Cook in 1975. Evans's book, though primarily a biography, contains considerable critical comment on the novels and relates their composition and their reception to the events in her life. The other three focus primarily on the novels. Considering their brevity, particularly the pamphlet length of the books by Edmonds and Graver, these three clarify incisively such characteristics of McCullers' fiction as her recurring themes, her patterns of imagery, her settings, and her alleged strengths and weaknesses as an artist.

Oliver Evans's view that McCullers' didacticism relates to that of Hawthorne and Melville in the tradition of American literature conflicts with Graver's view of McCullers as simply a writer "of bright and melancholy moods" rather than a philosopher capable of commenting on social and intellectual issues. While Edmonds and Graver agree—as do I—that *The Ballad of the Sad Cafe* and *The Member of the Wedding* are her best works, they disagree as to which of her first two novels, *The Heart Is a Lonely Hunter* or *Reflections in a Golden Eye*, is better. Edmonds, Graver, and Cook all conclude, more certainly than I would, that the last of McCullers' novels, *Clock Without Hands*, fails. Both Graver and Cook suggest that McCullers' accomplishment in the short story and in poetry is trivial; Edmonds, on the other hand, thinks about half of her stories are notable, but he lacks space to analyze them and to comment specifically on them. I view the poems and stories as worthy of more attention than they have received. They contradict generalizations that are popular with the critics who take broad approaches to McCullers' fiction. The generalizations have some validity. But in the stories or poems we do not find freaks present to any notable extent, nor handicapped persons, nor

Southern settings, nor black characters, nor themes related to unrequited love. Even human isolation is seldom the main theme in the stories as it is in the novels. In the stories McCullers reveals certain dominant characteristics: she creates notable children and adolescents; she is absorbed with family crises, particularly those related to alcoholic violence; she has recourse to allegory; she focuses on the drama inherent in a single scene with only a few characters present; and she experiments considerably with tone—modulating from deep gloom through satiric humor to light-hearted comedy.

The poems, though few, range from the brief and highly compressed lyric to an expansive philosophical cycle, the chief themes of which are the origin of the human being, his fundamental nature, the nature of God, the mystery of evil, and the complexities of fate and free choice. More attention to the lesser-known writings of McCullers reveals the versatility and virtuosity of an author who wrote well in forms other than the novel—the short story, the novella, the play, the film script, the essay, and the poem.

The largest outpouring of critical essays about her has occurred at three points: in 1940, with the publication of the first novel, *The Heart Is a Lonely Hunter;* in the early 1950s, with the success of the play *The Member of the Wedding* and the appearance of the omnibus volume of novels and stories called *The Ballad of the Sad Cafe and Other Works* (1951); and finally, in 1961 with the publication of *Clock Without Hands*, fifteen years after the appearance of her fourth novel. If these three bursts of attention marked McCullers' career, in almost no year after 1940 has there been an absence of criticism of her work.

Except for *Clock Without Hands*, her novels have remained steadily in print, and all but the last novel have become motion pictures or stage plays. Margarita Smith, Carson McCullers' sister, edited a selection of miscellaneous uncollected sketches, stories, essays, and poems, *The Mortgaged Heart* (1971), which has done much to consolidate her reputation. In 1976 there appeared the most complete annotated bibliography of writings on McCullers— *Carson McCullers and Katherine Anne Porter*, edited by Robert F. Kiernan.

In 1975 Virginia Spencer Carr in *The Lonely Hunter* presented a detailed and fascinating portrait of this author who suffered greatly, but who achieved more than one would have thought possible. The genius revealed in the work produced in about eight years, before she reached the age of thirty, intensifies the magnitude of the tragedy of her disabling illness, when she was in the midst of producing so much first-rate work and experimenting with so many forms. The loss to literature was great when she became ill, yet her twenty years of debilitating suffering do not diminish, but make more remarkable, her total achievement. V. S. Pritchett in 1955 called her "the best American novelist in a generation"; Walter Allen in *The Modern Novel in Britain and the United States* (1964) saw her, apart from Faulkner, as "the most remarkable novelist the South has produced"; Tennessee Williams consistently praised her as a worker of miracles; and Gore Vidal called her "the greatest and most lasting of the Southern Writers." A decade after her death, such praise seems hardly overstated when one considers her best work and the range of her total work. Her achievement is substantial, individual, and impressive. Her work deserves continuing analysis, interpretation, and commentary because of its incisiveness, its comprehensiveness, its sophistication, and its craft.

Acknowledgments

I wish to thank my husband, Frederick P. W. McDowell, for his reading and criticism of this book and for his encouragement. I also wish to thank my research assistant, Judy Lensink, for her careful reading and re-reading of the manuscript, and the Graduate College of the University of Iowa for financial assistance in the typing of the manuscript.

For permission to quote from the works of McCullers, acknowledgment is made to Houghton Mifflin Company, publishers of the following works from which excerpts are reprinted:

Reflections in a Golden Eye, copyright © renewed 1968 by Floria V. Lasky.

The Ballad of the Sad Cafe, Copyright 1951 by Carson McCullers.

The Member of the Wedding, Copyright 1946 by Carson McCullers © renewed 1974 by Floria Lasky.

Clock Without Hands, Copyright © 1961 by Carson McCullers.

Wunderkind, Copyright 1936 by Carson McCullers.

Madame Zilensky and the King of Finald, Copyright 1941 by Carson McCullers.

The Mortgaged Heart, Copyright 1971 by Floria Lasky.

Chronology

1917   February 19, Lulu Carson Smith born, Columbus, Georgia, to Marguerite Waters Smith and Lamar Smith.

1926 -   Studies piano; practices six to eight hours daily; may have
1934   abandoned concert aspirations before 1932.

1930   Changes name to *Carson*. Begins piano study with Mary Tucker at Fort Benning.

1932   Suffers pneumonia and undiagnosed rheumatic fever.

1934   Spring, Mary Tucker leaves. Fall, Carson moves to New York.

1934 -   Studies writing in evenings at Columbia University and
1936   New York University. Meets Reeves McCullers. Makes trips home to Georgia because of several illnesses.

1937 -   Marries; lives in Charlotte, North Carolina, and Fay-
1938   etteville, North Carolina; contract and $500 advance from publisher for *The Mute*.

1939   April, completes *The Mute*. Writes *Army Post*. Returns twice to Columbus alone.

1940   *The Heart Is a Lonely Hunter* (June). To New York. Meets Annemarie Clarac-Schwarzenbach. August at Bread Loaf, Middlebury, Vermont. September, February House, Brooklyn Heights. October-November, *Reflections in a Golden Eye, Harpers Bazaar*.

1941   *Reflections in a Golden Eye* (February). Mild stroke. David Diamond, Carson, and Reeves have complicated love affair. June at Yaddo, Saratoga, New York. Fall, initiates divorce. Returns to Columbus. Critical illness.

1942   "A Tree, A Rock, A Cloud," *Harpers Bazaar; O. Henry's Prize Stories*. After divorce, Reeves reenlists. Guggenheim Fellowship. Yaddo for six months.

1943   *The Ballad of the Sad Cafe, Harpers Bazaar* (August). $1,000 grant from American Academy of Arts and Letters.

1944   *The Ballad of the Sad Cafe* in Foley's *Best American Short Stories*. Reeves wounded twice. Father dies. Mother, Rita, and Carson move to Nyack, New York.

1945   Remarries Reeves, who is discharged and hospitalized. Summer at Yaddo.

1946   *The Member of the Wedding* (March). Second Guggenheim Fellowship. In June to Nantucket to see Tennessee Williams and to dramatize *The Member of the Wedding*. In November to Paris with Reeves.

1947   Strokes, August and November—blindness, loss of speech, permanent paralysis of left side. December, Reeves and Carson both flown by air ambulance to New York hospital; Reeves afflicted with severe alcoholism.

1948   *Mademoiselle* Merit Award. Suicide attempt.

1950   *The Member of the Wedding* opens January 5 for 501 performances. Receives New York Drama Critics Circle Award, Donaldson Annual Award for Best Drama, and Gold Medal of Theatre Club, Inc. for best playwright of year. Sees Elizabeth Bowen in Ireland, Tuckers in Virginia, and Edith Sitwell in New York.

1951   *The Ballad of the Sad Cafe and Other Works* (Omnibus Edition). Film version of *The Member of the Wedding*.

1952   With Reeves, buys home outside Paris. "The Dual Angel" in *Mademoiselle* and in *Botteghe Oscure*.

1953   "The Pestle," *Mademoiselle*. Plans divorce. Reeves commits suicide in France, November.

1954   February-May, lecture appearances with Tennessee Williams. April-July, at Yaddo.

1955   Mother dies suddenly.

1957   *The Square Root of Wonderful* on Broadway for forty-five performances.

1958   *The Square Root of Wonderful*, with preface.

1958 - 1962   Suffers severe illnesses and undergoes surgery for breast cancer and for atrophied hand muscles. Supported by psychiatric care of Dr. Mary Mercer in depressive illness, 1958; supported by her friendship the rest of her life.

1959   Meets Isak Dinesen in New York.

1961   *Clock Without Hands*.

1963 - 1964   Edward Albee's dramatization of *The Ballad of the Sad Cafe*, 123 performances. Fractures right hip and left elbow. *Sweet as a Pickle, Clean as a Pig* (children's poems).

1965   Hip surgery. Long critical illness.

1967   Film version of *Reflections in a Golden Eye*. August 15, stroke, followed by coma until death, September 29. Buried in Oak Hill Cemetery, Nyack.

1968   Film version of *The Heart Is a Lonely Hunter.*
1971   *The Mortgaged Heart,* edited by sister, Margarita Smith.

CHAPTER 1

Development of the Writer and Her Theory of Fiction

I McCullers' Emergence as a Southern Writer

CARSON McCullers' achievement lay in her remarkable versatility. Though illness limited her productivity after she was about thirty, she had already won critical and popular approbation in several literary genres—the novel, the novella, the short story, and the drama, including adaptations of her works of fiction. Of lesser consequence, she composed a few philosophical poems that hold autobiographical interest and that reveal her ability to write experimentally and to organize works around metaphysical symbols. Her sister suggested in a prefatory note to *The Mortgaged Heart*, published after Carson's death, that while Carson began with plays and novels and wrote poems only when she had become an established author, she was essentially a poet and a musician in all the prose that she wrote.[1]

The symbolical richness of her prose is perhaps the quality that most associates it with poetry. In her fiction she developed metaphysical themes with subtlety, eliciting with firmness and insight their symbolic, allegorical, and philosophical ramifications. The effects she creates are often startling, as she develops the far-reaching intonations of situations that might otherwise seem only melodramatic or sensational. Her flair for the grotesque and its symbolical overtones only partly obscures, however, a consistent sympathy for the lonely human being; and her regret that selfless love is rare and apt to be evanescent is intense in every book.

Carson McCullers is a master also of realistic narrative, revealing much insight into the tangled inner lives of human beings and

15

much knowledge of the Southern social scene of the 1940s. Especially noteworthy is her ability to perceive the complex gradations existing between the ordinary and the neurotic elements in personality and the relationships existing between so-called normal people and ostensibly abnormal ones. Her most extreme characters call attention to qualities universally present, but often unacknowledged, in human personality.

Sexual deviation and violent sexual antagonism function in her work, therefore, both as social fact and as symbolic states. Racial fear and hatred, psychotic isolation, and uncertainty about the norms and the significance of sexual expression produce the crises in her fiction. In it, physical malformations such as giantism and dwarfism, physical asymmetry and imbalance (crossed eyes, eyes of two colors, masculine characteristics in a woman or feminine characteristics in a male), are both realistic elements in characterization and abnormalities with philosophical significance. At its most intense, fascination with the grotesque appears as a predilection for cruelty to animals or for humanlike animals in *Reflections in a Golden Eye*. Superstition and folk legend also hover over McCullers' fictional universe: the suggestions of witchcraft, for example, in Miss Amelia's magic potions and the weird struggle between the vengeful man and the female giant in *The Ballad of the Sad Cafe*. But if McCullers focuses on unusual people and bizarre circumstances, she also, upon occasion, reveals a consummate and delicate mastery of more typical human experience, as in her poignant and humorous depictions of adolescent uncertainty in *The Member of the Wedding*.

McCullers maintained that an author always reflects the region of his birth and cannot escape his or her geographical area with its "voices and foliage and memory." Consequently, she regarded all of her major works as Southern. McCullers returned frequently to the South, but she admitted that she always found herself involved in arguments there, in "a stirring up of love and antagonism." Regardless of her liberal politics and her early longing to escape to New York, she found she could not separate herself in her work from the "homeland." She was, she thought, like most Southern writers, "bound to this particular regionalism."[2] It was her conviction that few Southern writers could ever become truly cosmopolitan in the sense, at least, of uprooting themselves completely from a cultural tradition.

Her family history, as well as her own childhood and adolescence, deepened her relationship with the South. Her ancestors on both sides of the family had been Southerners for generations, and ultimately contributed their part to the Southern ambience of her fiction. Her maternal grandmother arrived in Columbus, Georgia, as a young widow with four small children only a few months before she gave birth to Marguerite Waters, who was to become Carson's mother. The widow's brother, already a resident of Columbus, provided a house for the family, where, in fact, Lulu Carson Smith— later Carson McCullers—was born a generation later, on February 19, 1917. Carson McCullers' father, Lamar Smith, the youngest of ten children in an Alabama farming family, was only six when his father died. He came to Columbus as a young man to take a job as a watchmaker in the jewelry store that he eventually owned. (John Singer in *The Heart Is a Lonely Hunter* and Frankie Addams' father in *The Member of the Wedding* work in jewelry stores.) It was in this store that Carson's father met her mother, for she was also employed there, and it was in this store that he was found dead one night in the 1940s.

While in all her work McCullers focuses on alienated individuals, she herself grew up in a harmonious family. Her father saved all his Sundays for family outings and earned the love and respect of his children. Marguerite Waters Smith, her mother, assumed—and publicly proclaimed—almost from the day of Carson's birth that she was destined for fame—probably on the concert stage. Marguerite's friends regarded her as an outgoing woman, whose sense of humor and intelligence allowed her to adapt to any individual or group. Warmly maternal, she promoted Carson's sense of well-being by accepting her eccentricities in adolescence and later, instead of criticizing them. She was easygoing with her other two children as well. As to her children's friends, she regarded them with affection and looked upon Reeves McCullers, Carson's husband, as still one more of her children. She also enjoyed her reputation as a woman with a phenomenal memory. Whenever Marguerite seemed preoccupied, her friends joked that she was memorizing *War and Peace*, because she occasionally demonstrated her ability to recite the first chapter of that novel.[3]

Like the child in her first-published story, "Wunderkind," Carson throughout childhood and adolescence lived so intensively with her ambition to become a concert pianist that music seemed to her more real than the people she came to know and the region in which she grew up. Like Frances, the child in her story, she also experienced frustration and inner exhaustion in her drive to achieve both technical mastery and sensitivity of interpretation. While still

in elementary school, according to neighbors, she sometimes practiced three hours early in the morning and another three to five
hours after school. Between the ages of thirteen and eighteen she
studied with Mary Tucker, a concert pianist whose husband was
stationed at Fort Benning, near Columbus. For five years Carson
spent all day Saturday at the Tucker home, being instructed or
playing with the Tuckers' daughter between lessons. Her relationships with this family were crucial for her. During her adolescence,
she gradually identified herself with the Tuckers, and through the
imaginative stimulus that they exercised over her, she widened her
intellectual horizons to appreciate cultures other than her own.

Like Frances, the prodigy in "Wunderkind," McCullers had
auditioned for her teacher by playing Liszt's Second Hungarian
Rhapsody with great verve but with little sense of modulation or of
interpretive finesse. In spite of such relevant details, McCullers discounted autobiographical interpretations of this story. She noted
particularly the difference between Mary Tucker and the crotchety
Herr Bilderbach, Frances' teacher. But the autobiographical echoes
are obvious. Fifteen-year-old Frances gives up the piano one winter
afternoon because, although technically skillful, she cannot interpret music the way she feels it. The situation reflects McCullers'
own emotional fatigue and her concern at having to disappoint a
demanding but greatly admired teacher. Her decision to forego a
concert career was probably made shortly before she wrote this
story at the age of seventeen.

Mick Kelly in *The Heart Is a Lonely Hunter* reflects less convincingly than does Frances in "Wunderkind" Carson McCullers'
passion for musical achievement and for music itself. Mick attempts
to build a violin; she appreciates music heard from open windows of
the lucky families who own radios; and she tries to learn to play the
piano in the school gym. Her lesser talent and sophistication
separate her experience from that of the prodigy, Frances, and from
the more gifted McCullers, but Mick is also the victim of circumstances which prevent her from at least trying to become a musician. She has every confidence in her ability, and there is never any
notion in her own mind that she would not be successful if she
could only afford to study. Her faith that she may someday be able
to go back to school and study music, in fact, organizes her thinking
and makes her defy every discouragement at the end of the novel.

Considerable biographical significance must be attached to
McCullers' acknowledgment that the intensity informing *The*

Member of the Wedding represented her mature "working through" of old adolescent conflicts and regrets.[4] The book centers on Frankie Addams' determination to attain an identity that transcends the self. Paradoxically, while she seeks community "with all the people in the world," she is, like a typical adolescent, rebellious and anxious to define the elements of a new self. Frankie seeks union with her brother and his bride—and through them with all mankind—so that her own exciting "future" can begin. At several points in the background of this novel, a piano tuner plays scales over and over, leaving the last note unstruck. Frankie is convinced that her sense of the need to complete the scale will drive her mad. A compelling blues tune, interrupted just before a phrase is finished, also haunts her with the feeling that something is about to happen but for some reason does not. The world is standing still. The communion with others which Frankie seeks resembles the sense of completion which Carson briefly and tentatively found with the Tuckers when she was Frankie's age. Despite her pronounced sense of alienation, rapport with others was always vital to Carson, even in her relationships with people whom she had just met or whom she knew primarily through their writing. This search for a closely shared identity often became a compulsive possessiveness for someone whom she admired or loved.

When Carson left Columbus for New York at seventeen, she may still have intended to study at the Julliard School of Music, but, more likely, she had firmly decided against a musical career during her last year of high school. She did not tell Mary Tucker that she had made this decision until she learned in the spring of 1934 that the Tuckers were moving. In any event, an impassioned concern to read and write made her determine to read every book of consequence in the Columbus Public Library during the year after high-school graduation. She later called the library her "spiritual home." During this year she also wrote at least one short story, "Sucker," in which an adolescent boy, preoccupied with his wish for recognition by an adolescent girl, rejects a younger child for whom he had felt protective affection. The story foreshadows an emotional conflict repeated in later works, the incessant stress between adolescent and younger child, a preoccupation McCullers more fully charts in the relationships between Mick Kelly and Bubber in *The Heart Is a Lonely Hunter* and between Frankie Addams and John Henry in *The Member of the Wedding*. In both novels, a sense of guilt and loss follows the young girl's realization that she has outgrown her psychic dependence upon a child for whom she still sometimes feels affectionate comradeship.

Life in New York in 1934 was for Carson a period of loneliness, but also of intellectual challenge. Although she later declared that she read books in phone booths to avoid crowds of strangers, she was friendly and unusually self-confident and self-assertive in her relationships with others. She seems actually to have suffered little from the shyness which many young strangers feel when they leave a small town for a large city. Until 1937 she held a series of inconsequential jobs, while she studied fiction writing in the evenings at Columbia University. She seems to have had some initial success when Whit Burnett, one of her teachers and editor of *Story*, purchased two of her stories, "Like That" and "Wunderkind," for publication. Occasionally, she was forced to return to Columbus to convalesce from debilitating respiratory illnesses and undiagnosed heart disease.

Her ill-fated, yet inspiriting marriage opened up a new world of experience for Carson McCullers, and the complexities of her marital situation are, of course, reflected in various ways in her fiction. She met Reeves McCullers, an army sergeant, in Columbus in 1936, and after he left military service that fall he returned to New York with her to study creative writing at Columbia University. He dropped out of the university when Carson again became ill and had to be taken back to Georgia. In September 1937, at the height of the Depression, they married and settled first in Charlotte and then in Fayetteville, North Carolina. While Carson wrote, Reeves postponed his university education and his career as a writer. Working on a commission basis, he collected overdue accounts for a credit agency.

From the first, Carson revealed the discipline which was to characterize her practice of the craft of fiction, as it had characterized her determination to excel in music, by maintaining a rigorous working schedule. But she did not altogether neglect the responsibilities of domestic life, and she attended to them with good humor. It was her practice, for instance, to empty waste cans with musical accompaniment appropriate to their contents: "I always half shut my eyes and begin singing—usually something militant and tremendous like the funeral march from Götterdämmerung (making a final clash with the top of the can for the kettledrums and cymbals). . . . For the waste basket . . . filled mostly with literary miscarriages, a light airy bit of Schubert or Haydn will do."[5]

Literary recognition came early for McCullers. In 1938 she received an advance on royalties from Houghton Mifflin for her projected novel *The Mute*, later named by her publishers *The Heart Is a Lonely Hunter*. When the book was published in early summer 1940, Carson and her husband returned to New York where publishers, reviewers, and other novelists applauded her at the age of twenty-three as the literary discovery of the year. She was immediately invited to be a fellow that summer at the Bread Loaf Writers Conference in Vermont. *Reflections in a Golden Eye*, which she had written in two months and which she had not expected to publish, was soon scheduled to appear that fall in *Harpers Bazaar* before its publication as a book. While still in her twenties, she received two Guggenheim awards. For *The Ballad of the Sad Cafe*, printed serially in 1943 and as a book in 1944, she won a thousand-dollar prize from the American Academy of Letters, and she received for *The Member of the Wedding* in 1948 the *Mademoiselle* Merit Award. Her first four novels appeared within six years; all of her books sold over half a million copies.

Her greatest public acclaim came with the stage production of *The Member of the Wedding*, which ran for 501 performances in New York beginning in January 1950, starring Julie Harris and Ethel Waters. In 1950 she received the New York Drama Critics Circle Award, the Donaldson Award for best drama of the year, and the Gold Medal of the Theatre Club, Inc. for best playwright of the year. At the close of the first decade of her career she loomed as a figure of central importance in American literature. Soon she developed friendships with well-known intellectuals and writers. Writers like Louis Untermeyer early recognized her promise as they worked with her at Bread Loaf and at the Yaddo Writers Colony in the early 1940s. Tennessee Williams, Dame Edith Sitwell, Elizabeth Bowen, and Baroness Karen Blixen (Isak Dinesen) knew her first through her work and then sought or welcomed her friendship as a fellow writer. Her well-known friends included Edward Albee, Muriel Rukeyser, and Truman Capote. Still other people of note in literature and the arts lived at February House in Brooklyn Heights, her home for the war years while she and Reeves were divorced and he was again in military service. In 1940 George Davis of *Mademoiselle* purchased this house; W. H. Auden managed it. Residents included W. H. Auden, Christopher Isherwood, Louis MacNeice, Richard Wright, Erica and Klaus Mann (children of Thomas Mann), Benjamin Britten, Peter Pears, and Gypsy Rose

Lee. Salvador Dali, Anaïs Nin, and Leonard Bernstein dropped in at the house as visitors. McCullers lived here from time to time from autumn 1940 until 1945.

If fame and achievement came early to the young writer who had seemed destined to be a concert pianist, so also did personal stress, which deepened into tragedy. After a four-year marriage, Carson McCullers divorced Reeves McCullers when she was twenty-four and newly famous. He reentered the army, and she worried intensely about his safety during the war years. They remarried four years later in 1945. After another eight years, at the age of thirty-six, Carson was in the United States planning a second divorce when Reeves killed himself in France. His frustrated writing ambitions, his debilitating alcoholism and Carson's own heavy drinking, as well as her illnesses, eventual invalidism, and paralysis, all contributed to the complications, suffering, and turbulence of their lives. Both were bisexual. Carson, however, even as a young woman, confided to friends that she was often too exhausted by repeated illness to engage in sexual intercourse.

Before her divorce, Carson McCullers experienced frustration in her love for a woman, as well as in her love for Reeves. When Reeves and Carson McCullers arrived in New York in the early summer of 1940, Carson fell in love almost immediately with Annemarie Clarac-Schwarzenbach, a free-lance Swiss writer and a friend of the Thomas Mann family. She had lived through several years of danger, smuggling people threatened with political imprisonment out of Germany. Though Carson's love for Annemarie was frustrated almost from the beginning, Annemarie pointedly avoided hurting the younger woman more than necessary.Annemarie, who was married, was already in love with another woman, and she refused Carson's insistent pleading that they meet in Boston and vacation together at Cape Cod. Nevertheless, Carson's fascination remained strong during the summer that she was spending at Bread Loaf in 1940. As an indication of her devotion to Annemarie Clarac-Schwarzenbach, she dedicated her second novel, *Reflections in a Golden Eye,* to her when it appeared in *Harpers Bazaar* in the fall of 1940. In 1942 she suffered intense grief when she received word of Annemarie's sudden death in Europe after months of mental illness and drug addiction.

Carson McCullers' most productive period followed in the first half of the 1940s. In the fall of 1940 she temporarily left Reeves and moved into February House. Though her personal life was far from placid in these years, she wrote diligently while she lived at February House and at Yaddo Colony in Saratoga, New York, where she benefited from the strict rules against her being interrupted at her typewriter. The fruits of these years were her third and fourth novels, *The Ballad of the Sad Cafe* and *The Member of the Wedding*. She began writing *The Member of the Wedding* in 1940 (calling it *The Bride*) but turned from it to write *The Ballad of the Sad Cafe*, which obliquely reflects a brief, but intense, triangular love affair with David Diamond. Diamond, a young composer and violinist, met Carson and Reeves at the home of Muriel Rukeyser in the spring of 1941 and immediately declared that he was in love with both of them. Reeves apparently loved both Carson and Diamond, while Carson loved Reeves, Diamond, and Annemarie.

A factor that may have contributed to her confused social and sexual life was her talent for making remarkably close friendships very quickly. Her open and direct manner shocked some and greatly attracted others. The complexity of her emotional entanglements contrasts with the apparent simplicity of her devotion and responsiveness to strangers like Diamond or Annemarie. Diamond wrote the night he met Carson, "This amazing child and woman is a part of me." Many friends at this time, including Louis Untermeyer, reflected similarly on her childlike charm and appearance. A day later Diamond wrote, "I know . . . I love these two human beings." The following day he added, "Since last night I think only of Carson and Reeves and the way Reeves looked at me." Diamond was unable to drink as heavily as Carson and Reeves and found himself shocked at the violence of their quarrels. Carson told Diamond of her continuing great love for Annemarie. Nevertheless, Diamond assumed that Carson would soon divorce Reeves, and he hoped she would then marry him.[6]

In the summer of 1941, Carson worked at Yaddo on *The Ballad of the Sad Cafe*, a novel which dramatizes a strange love affair of two men and a woman and incorporates elements of folklore. The tall female in this book is defeated in physical combat by her hated ex-husband only because her new beloved, a dwarf, becomes his ally. Diamond knew that the novel about the strange triangle would be dedicated to him when it was completed, and he also knew that, after it appeared in *Harpers Bazaar,* the manuscript would be his property.

If, in the weeks at Yaddo with Diamond, Carson experienced much sexual confusion and disillusionment, frustration of another

sort developed when Katherine Anne Porter rebuffed her when she
made overtures of friendship and expressed admiration for her and
her work. Porter was apparently more concerned with helping her
protégée Eudora Welty—also at Yaddo—become established. Diamond had the previous summer become acquainted with Katherine
Anne Porter and now enjoyed her friendship, frequently eating his
meals with her. He left Yaddo during the summer. First continuing
his work at the MacDowell Colony, he later returned to New York
and lived with Reeves McCullers. In the meantime, Carson had
completed *The Ballad of the Sad Cafe,* with its dedication to Diamond. In November Diamond dedicated his new ballet to both
Reeves and Carson, and in December he set to music Carson's
poem "The Twisted Trinity."

Still other personal complications clouded the six years in which
McCullers' fame rapidly grew with the publication of her first four
books. In 1942, Annemarie suddenly died. Late in 1941 Carson
divorced Reeves, and he reenlisted in 1942 in the army. Constantly
worried about his safety in the war, Carson hesitated to work at her
favorite retreat, Yaddo, because of a premonition that she would be
notified there about his death as she had learned while there about
Annemarie's. Twice in 1944 she was informed that he had been
wounded. Also in 1944 in Georgia she struggled unsuccessfully to
help her father stop drinking. He was found dead in his jewelry
store at night that summer; the coroner ruled the death a heart attack. In 1945 Carson left February House, and with her mother and
sister, Rita, who now worked at *Mademoiselle,* she established a
home at Nyack, New York. Though Carson also maintained an
apartment in the city and remarried Reeves in 1945, she frequently
needed the steadying influence and the nursing care provided by
her mother.

Carson's health tragically restricted her, even in the first decade
of her career. In her adolescence she had apparently contracted
rheumatic fever, and in her maturity she suffered three strokes, the
aftereffects of the disease. Her first stroke in 1941 temporarily affec-
ted her eyesight, while the trauma of her second, suffered in France
one night in August 1947, while Reeves was hospitalized for treatment of a war injury, haunted her the rest of her life. She lay on the
floor, fully conscious, for over eight hours, unable to move or cry for
help. This stroke left her face numb and caused a loss of lateral vision in the right eye and a partial paralysis of her left side. In
November 1947 a third stroke, with a hemorrhage on the right side

of the brain, permanently paralyzed her left side. After three weeks, both Carson and Reeves were flown by ambulance to a New York hospital. (Reeves, who was being treated for acute alcoholism, suf fered withdrawal symptoms and delirium tremens on the trip.) Carson could never again play the piano, type, or even turn pages without difficulty. Only after many months of therapy did she learn to walk with a cane. As muscles in her hand and arm atrophied, she lost the ability to sign her name.

Even with her illnesses, McCullers had achieved remarkable success between the ages of twenty-three and thirty. Though she continued to write, as an invalid, until her death at fifty, her creative activity was necessarily lessened. As her muscles lost strength and her joints stiffened, she underwent many operations to increase physical agility and to lessen pain. She needed two operations to set and reset a fractured hip; four heart operations to prevent further strokes; and a mastectomy after breast cancer set in. Repeatedly, she was hospitalized for pneumonia. Only once was she so completely depressed as to attempt suicide.

Illness did not completely impede her literary activity, and her sufferings became a part of her work. She wrote short articles for magazines, a play, *The Square Root of Wonderful* (1958), and a novel, *Clock Without Hands* (1961). In the novel, J. T. Malone faces death for a year after learning he has leukemia. McCullers records his experience with the validity that only an author who has adjusted, through various stages of resentment and despair, to suffering, disability, and early death could achieve. In her suffering and her courage, her mother's care sustained her until 1955. After 1958 the companionship and care of her psychiatrist and close friend, Dr. Mary Mercer, supported her.

II *McCullers' Views on the Art of Fiction*

Carson McCullers seldom articulated her aesthetic theory. She seemed too busy experimenting with her craft and too absorbed in her characters to do much abstract thinking about the practice of fiction: "The ingenuities of aesthetics have never been my problems," she wrote. "Flight, in itself, interests me and I am indifferent to salting the bird's tail."[7] The principles of her craft she had discovered, to some extent, by trial and error as she worked systematically and intensively. Each work, when completed, revealed her imaginative fecundity and her firm control of her sub-

ject, but she seldom saw either her plots or her characters clearly
when she began to work on a novel. Her novels grew slowly and unpredictably, until her imagination would finally release her to a
broader understanding of the people before her, their motivations,
and their relationships. This uncertain evolution of her fiction she
saw as peculiar to her, not as a process necessarily applicable to
other authors. While her personal life seems often erratic and uncontrolled, her career as author reveals remarkable discipline. Accordingly, in her early writing years she resented interruptions during her long hours at the typewriter, much as she had resented interruptions during her long hours at the piano.

Though she often felt that facts would "impede intuition" in her
own creative enterprises, still she recognized the role of intellect
(even if it were for her secondary) in the artistic process: "Writing is
a wandering, dreaming occupation. The intellect is submerged
beneath the unconscious—the thinking mind is best controlled by
the imagination." Longing for her prose to emerge suffused with
the "light of poetry,"[8] she distrusted her own tendencies to use full
documentary detail in recounting an event, to reproduce regional
dialect, and to sketch in the Southern landscape. She reveals her independence of social realities as such and her ability to imagine
characters independently of an exact knowledge of their everyday
lives in her use of John Singer in her first novel, *The Heart Is a
Lonely Hunter*. She had herself never known a deaf-mute, but
made of John Singer a convincing character. To show her independence of actual fact in the creative process, she refused to attend a
nearby convention of deaf-mutes, because confrontation of such a
reality might alter her imaginative conception of Singer, which by
this time satisfied her.

This novel also reveals the wayward and unplanned nature of her
activity as a writer. Singer had already undergone several unfore-
seen alterations, even in his very name. At first, all the characters in
her as yet unnamed book sought out a Jewish businessman, Harry
Minowitz, to confide in him their hopes, plans, and griefs. Although
the entire structure of the novel centered on the magnetic
Minowitz, McCullers herself could not understand why all her other
people gravitated toward him. Later, she declared that she worked
for a whole year without understanding the book at all and had
almost decided to break it into short stories, since she could not find
in it a clear design or thematic unity.

Then, typical of her activity as writer, she suddenly saw the
significance of Harry Minowitz, changed his name, and envisioned

him as John Singer, a deaf-mute engraver of jewelry. With this unexplained flash of intuition, she realized what John Singer should do
in her novel: he was neither to hear nor react to anything said to
him and in turn no one to whom he listened would actually want his
advice.[9] After several years of frustrated work on "The Bride," the
first form of *The Member of the Wedding*, McCullers had a similar
abrupt revelation: Frankie Addams wanted to be the third party in
her brother's wedding. Around Frankie's obsessive wish, McCullers'
short—and subtly autobiographical—novel suddenly fell into
focus.[10]

Because of such experiences in writing her own fiction, McCullers
advised other writers to plunge into their work in partial ignorance
of their aesthetic predispositions. Few creative writers either anticipate or comprehend the dimensions of a given work until it is
finished. She was convinced that illuminations incrementally arise
in the imaginations of many authors only during rigorous labor on
their manuscripts. Foreign to her was the passive sort of inspiration
that dominates the aesthetics of romanticism. Rather, for her, the
"grace of labor" was all-important, the work developing through
the tension established between one's labor and the unconscious.[11]

When she was working daily on *Clock Without Hands* and
predicted the book would require two more years of effort, she
emphasized not only the need for hard work but the fact that hard
work was not enough. An illumination had to strike her in order for
her work to have focus and balance—but such illumination was
never available to her until she had worked days and even years on
a given work. She saw fiction as a "foreshortening of memory" and
used her own experience to help her identify with that of her
characters. Thus, the characters eventually built a story in her imagination which became to her "truer than reality" but was informed by her own memories.

In "Wunderkind" she illustrates the writer's use of his or her experience, modulated and transformed. Similarly, in *The Member of
the Wedding*, with its autobiographical basis, the bizarre nature of
Frankie Addams' insistence on accompanying her brother and his
bride on their honeymoon belongs to fiction, but Frankie's dreams
of "belonging" and her traumatic sense of being left behind or
abandoned as an adolescent lay in McCullers' memory.

McCullers could never analyze the "illumination," "the divine
spark," or the "divine collusion" which gave focus to her work. It
was to her a forging of "the dream and the logic of God." The sudden imaginative light which she counted on coming to her in the

course of each book would be the result, she felt, of long preliminary labor on each manuscript. Obviously, the adolescent girls obsessed with music are the characters one most easily associates with the author. But she insisted that she identified herself imaginatively with every person in her work and for the moment became that person—male and female, white and black, homosexual and heterosexual, child and adult. In her journals she asked, "How can you create a character without love and the struggle that goes with love?" She declared firmly, "When I write about a deaf-mute, I become dumb."[12]

Some of McCullers' most fully developed statements on literary theory relate to the drama. In these, she returns repeatedly to discussion of her central themes—frustration when love is not available, the universality of isolation, the relationship between "moral isolation" and evil, and love either as a cure for loneliness or as an intensifier of loneliness. In the process of becoming human, an infant must, McCullers explained in "Loneliness . . . an American Malady," first become aware of its separateness and then it must also relate itself to "something larger and more powerful."[13] A child learns to identify himself through his connections with others. Ideally, love should provide the amalgamation through which the separate individual relates to another individual or to a group. If one asks, "Who am I?" and finds no answer through personal relationships with those who accept him, he will be vulnerable to fear, a primary source in McCullers' work of all evil. He then defines himself only in terms of what he is *not* and hates whatever is identified as "other," that is, those who are unlike him. Thoreau alone in the woods and Thomas Wolfe in city crowds discovered, in totally different environments, that what the individual thinks of himself or herself in relation to society will determine that individual's fate.[14]

In McCullers' novels the characters inadequately communicate their views and feelings to others, and, perhaps more importantly, they inadequately define or articulate for their own understanding their problems of identity and of relationship. The silent groping for solutions to both of these problems is symbolized in McCullers' first novel by her use of two deaf-mutes and by the suicide of the one who survives the death of the other. The theme of inadequate communication appears in *The Ballad of the Sad Cafe* in the limited dialogue, in the dependence on natural omens, and in much background whispering among the villagers. In *The Member of the Wedding* dialogue predominates, but it is unconnected, halting, and drifting, rather than connected logically, easily expressed, and moving toward conclusions or preconceived directions.

In writing on her techniques in experimenting with the drama, McCullers thought that the pioneering aspect of her play based on *The Member of the Wedding* lay in her return to a concern with characters as they embody abstractions and "inward conflicts."[15] Appearances matter less with these figures, because these characters exist primarily within their own psyches. The action in the play is "inward action" involving changes of moods, of directions, and of point of view—a kind of action one associates with poetry or with contemplative fiction, rather than with the drama. The audience may learn of these psychic shifts after they have taken place rather than at the time they occur. Parallel monologues sometimes substitute for actual dialogue, and seemingly unrelated stage business is engaged in by the characters when they are trying to think through a difficult abstraction. The play moves only as the characters become involved in a moral or metaphysical problem of importance to them—the meaning of time or of chance, the role of fate in their lives, their need for love, their ability or inability to find love, and the importance of courage as one encounters human existence.

McCullers defended the play against those who immediately criticized it as fragmentary and lacking in dramatic unity. Brooks Atkinson, for instance, reviewed it in the *New York Times* as a work which possesses "no beginning, middle, or end" and "never acquires dramatic momentum."[16] McCullers contended that such critics misunderstood the aesthetic concept of a drama whose design was intuitive. She felt also that she had achieved the unusual in this play in its lyricism and in its fusion of humor and grief, frequently within a single line. She believed that Harold Clurman, the director of the stage play and of the movie, understood her methods and saw that the "fugue-like parts" needed to be brought into "dazzling precision and harmony."[17] (One notices that McCullers in her critical statements on literature always returns to a vocabulary derived from music.)

So sure was she that she had composed in this play, as Tennessee Williams had in *The Glass Menagerie,* an unconventional drama, that she questioned whether this loose form for the expansion of her artistic vision should even be called a play. If her dramatic productions had some awkwardness in them, she wrote in 1950, even this should be forgiven as a necessary phase in the development of a new "mutation" in a genre. An art will die, she asserted, if it depends always on the traditional and conventional. She herself would willingly say to those who misunderstood her: "I seem strange to you, but anyway I am alive."[18]

The other theoretical subject upon which she wrote at length was the so-called "gothic" quality in much recent Southern fiction. Because she identified herself as a Southern writer, she became increasingly interested in the label "Southern gothic," which critics rather indiscriminately applied to Southern fiction. Unfortunately, her writing on this issue preceded publication of those works of her own which might be described as "gothic." In her first critical essay, "The Russian Realists and Southern Literature," she reacted against overuse of the term, because she thought that Southern fiction of her generation was rooted in realism and that "gothic" implied a romantic orientation with a dependence upon the supernatural incident or explanation, rather than upon the direct and courageous facing of the universe as it exists.[19] She developed in this essay the further idea that Russian realists of the nineteenth century and Southern realists of the twentieth had much in common, because both dealt with a region which maintained a "peasant" class and both could find in real life many people in their geographical area whose lives were worth no more than "a load of hay." In effect, she rejected in theory a kind of fiction which she was later to exemplify, at least in part of her work.

One would wish that McCullers had later developed more fully her views on the gothic in Southern literature, so that she could then have considered her own work like *Reflections in a Golden Eye* and more particularly *The Ballad of the Sad Cafe* in the light of such concepts. The closest we can find to such later writing are her essays on the gothic fiction of Isak Dinesen.[20]

CHAPTER 2

The Heart Is a Lonely Hunter *(1940)*

I *Isolation as Man's Fate*

T HE principal theme of *The Heart Is a Lonely Hunter* (1940), Carson McCullers declared, lay in the first dozen pages: an individual's compulsion to revolt against enforced isolation and his or her urge to express the self at all costs. She thought of the work in 1938, even in one of its earliest forms in *The Mute*, as consisting of variations on this principal concept. Thinking of her projected novel as analogous to a work of music, she enumerated in her proposal to Houghton Mifflin, five "counter-themes" that would, each of them, elaborate upon the central theme: the need for a person to create a unifying principle or god; the likelihood that any god that man creates will be chimerical or fantastic; the likely suppression by society of the individual; the deflection by social pressures of man's natural urge to cooperate with others; and the impressiveness of the heroism which occasionally appears in ordinary individuals. At times, these subsidiary themes would be obvious; at other times, they would be more difficult to define:

These themes are never stated nakedly in the book. Their overtones are felt through the characters and situations. Much will depend upon the insight of the reader and the care with which the book is read. In some parts the underlying ideas will be concealed far down below the surface of a scene and at other times these ideas will be shown with a certain emphasis.[1]

When she wrote her abstract in 1938, she had completed Part I of the novel, had worked for over a year on the book, and had already made drastic changes in her central characters. A principal change

31

from her projected plan is evident in the last section of the published novel. She had declared that, as with recurring motifs in a symphony, she would draw her major theme and all the counterthemes sharply together for an integrated finale. Actually, she did not do this.

Because her emphasis shifted as she worked on the novel, she gave greater importance by the end of the book to a young black woman, Portia Copeland, than she had first intended. Also thirteen-year-old Mick Kelly, one of the four characters originally envisioned as surrounding John Singer, develops more fully than the other three members. She becomes possibly even more significant in the novel than the mute, John Singer. McCullers' involvement with Portia and Mick modulates the pessimism of the concluding sequences of the book to a qualified optimism as these women reach out with some hope to the future. The finale was to have been one combining the four voices of Mick, Dr. Copeland, Biff Brannon, and Jeff Blount, as the death of Singer affects them deeply but draws them together harmoniously. Instead, Mick's voice rings in the finale above the voices of the other three, who remain locked in their despair. Mick has a vision of a future for herself, even if the way to fulfillment will be arduous. Portia, whose rancor against her father has been supplanted by a vision of self-sacrifice for the welfare of her father, her husband, and her brother, and who dreams of a simple, pastoral existence, complements the strident negation of the other characters. The ending intermingles a fleeting vision of a brighter future with the bleakness dominating the characters who react most intensely to Singer's suicide.

At the end of the short Part I, John Singer, a deaf-mute, mourns his separation from another deaf-mute, Antonapoulos, with whom he has lived. Singer has strongly opposed committing of the mentally retarded and overweight Antonapoulos to an asylum and has tried for months to conceal his friend's increasingly bizarre and mildly antisocial behavior. During the fourteen months covered by Part II—the major section of the novel—Singer lives in a shabby boarding house run by Mick Kelly's parents. His attentive silence and his thoughtful eyes draw four people close to him: Mick Kelly, a girl burdened by the care of two younger children, by poverty, and by frustration of her ambition to become a musician; Biff Brannon, who operates an all-night cafe; Jake Blount, an itinerant Marxist, who presently works for a carnival; and Dr. Benedict Mady Copeland, a proud and bitter black physician whose intense commitment to Marxism as the only means of raising the status of blacks has alienated him from most of his friends and relatives.

Though both Blount and Copeland are Marxist reformers and though Blount seeks to persuade Copeland to join him in overt political agitation, the two men differ greatly. Copeland resents the clumsy efforts at comradeship made by Blount, whose illiterate harangues are emotional and incite to physical violence. Blount even injures himself by beating his hands and head against a wall when Biff's customers in the restaurant ridicule his pleas for social change, for friendship, and for understanding among people. His speech registers only as the rantings of a drunk man. In turn, Dr. Copeland has his disappointments. He has to control his intense anger when his political talks at his Christmas party for blacks prove ineffective. When with great dignity he presents his annual scholarship to a gifted black youth, he seeks to persuade his listeners to engage in revolutionary action, but they simply nod or mutter "amen." He ends his day in his darkened parlor, exhausted and spiritually desolate. In his passion to bring about radical social change and to better his people, he alienates most of them and even his own family.

At the close of Part II, Antonapoulos dies, and Singer, in reaction to his loss, commits suicide. In Part III, the four people who have made Singer their confidant adjust to his death, still isolated from one another, and still lonely hunters for a selfless love and a spiritual understanding which eludes them. Throughout the novel, each of them talks uninhibitedly to Singer and imagines himself as understood completely by this man with alert, thoughtful eyes and intent attitude. Described by McCullers as "spokes" in a wheel—with Singer as the hub—the four do not grow closer to one another through their association with Singer. For example, when Singer buys a radio for his new friends to hear, they stand about awkwardly in his room, unable to converse with one another. Singer's response to the four is not the altogether intuitively wise one that they imagine it to be. In a letter to Antonapoulos, he expresses bewilderment, if not amusement, at the interest these people have displayed in him. Consequently, each character, except for Mick, is as defeated and isolated at the end of the book as at the beginning.

If Singer creates in his mind an illusory Antonapoulos who is worthy of his great love and grief, Biff, Jake, Mick, and Dr. Copeland create in Singer an illusory figure who possesses great virtue and wisdom. As such, he exists mostly in the imaginations of those who find in him solace and understanding. He is the god created as "unifying principle" and, as such, he is, in McCullers'

words, "chimerical and fantastic." The inability of Singer to speak
both symbolizes and dramatizes the lack of understanding and the
lack of communication among the characters. Ironically, the characters who are most articulate—Blount and Copeland—are no more
effective than Mick and Brannon. All fail to establish satisfying
social relationships as Portia Copeland is able to do. Both Jake
Blount, who wants to be a messiah for the workers, and Dr.
Copeland, the exponent of justice for blacks, are fanatical in their
one-sided vision, whenever they express their intensely held views
and try to find common cause with their listeners. Their fanaticism
undermines their sincere attempts to communicate with others and
to influence them.

If, in this first novel, McCullers presents love as the only available anodyne to isolation, none of her characters except Singer is
really unselfish enough to love others with entire sincerity. None of
them can love enough to deserve the love they crave. Singer does
love selflessly the retarded deaf-mute, who can only respond to affection instinctively, as a pet or a baby might. The attention Singer
offers to the other four characters appears to be love and is partly
love, yet he does not comprehend their needs fully nor do they
regard him as a person who might also need reassurance. They only
"sing" of their needs and thoughts to Singer, who, in spite of his
name, cannot really "sing" or express himself adequately.
Ironically, no true communication takes place between Singer and
his disciples, who all remain egoists. Singer inadvertently furthers
their narcissism by providing with his eyes the mirror wherein they
seem to see reflected what they themselves wish to see, irrespective
of whether he actually understands them.

Portia, Dr. Copeland's married daughter, who is a cook at the
Kellys' boarding house, loves generously, maternally, and uninhibitedly, but Portia, through much of the book, is less central
than the "quartet" and Singer. Portia's love also is sentimental to
the degree that it obscures the evil in the social order that threatens
the stability of her existence with her husband, Highboy, and with
her brother, Willie. A society motivated by prejudice prevents her
from building a secure relationship with her father, and it eventually even negates her hopes for the attainment of a pastoral happiness on her grandfather's small farm. Copeland and Blount both
express an abstract love for the working class and for blacks in their
efforts to secure social justice, but Blount simply ends up brawling
with laborers and Copeland has driven away even his family. Love

in McCullers' first novel is difficult to come by and is transient in most instances.

II   *The Quartet—the "Spokes of the Wheel"*

The quartet of people who surround Singer and become his disciples, as it were, are central in this novel. The least communicative of them is forty-four-year-old Biff Brannon, who, like Singer, is unemotional, disinterested, and observant. For eighteen years he has systematically collected in a back room of his cafe issues of the daily newspaper of the town, but he does not refer to the papers he saves. He never analyzes the news, but merely notices the day's happenings and then files each paper neatly and methodically. Similarly in his own life, Biff never philosophically integrates past, present, and future. He repeatedly recalls the same few memories but does not relate them to one another or to his life in the present. He only responds as necessary to individual, separate occurrences and never shapes his own life creatively through an active participation in the life surrounding him.

Typical of Biff's failure to connect incident and emotion is his and Alice's established mode of addressing each other as "Mr." and "Mrs."—a pattern begun impulsively years before, after a trivial argument. The distance implicit in such a mode of salutation also suggests the impersonal quality of their twenty-three-year marriage. For the reader, Alice remains in the background, as she probably does for Biff. In the early morning, Biff closes the restaurant and goes upstairs, as Alice arises, and they converse briefly. He neatly remakes the bed, undresses, and in his turn retires to sleep. Later in the day, at work in the cafe, they still remain remote as their lives routinely parallel but never merge. She supervises the workers while he handles the cash register and menus. Occasionally he wishes they had had children; he admires "Baby" Wilson, his pampered five-year-old niece, and he fantasizes at times about what life would be like if some of the Kelly children, particularly Mick, were his own.

Although Biff's anxieties are explicitly sexual, their exact nature remains a secret to the reader. The narrator makes what seem to be unconnected observations about Biff, and the reader is left to synthesize these remarks. Biff, like Singer, essentially observes the world but does not allow it to enter his life and change or reorganize it. The reader sees Biff, as he must perceive himself, as an unintegrated person. His social and private life, his intellect and emotion,

his marital relationship and his sexual life, his family life with his
mother and his present family life, his life upstairs in his apartment
and downstairs in the restaurant, his past, his present, and his
future—all are kept essentially separate. He organizes his time in
routine activities, but his inner life is completely composed of
separate parts never fitted together by an attempt to see himself as a
total human being.

For example, we learn of his sexual views at several different
points in the book. He is apparently impotent, at least with his wife,
and seems incapable of sustained and growing emotional relationships. Memory of his "godly" mother may inhibit him. At one point
long ago, he chivalrously defended Alice's sister against her
drunken husband, and he platonically enjoys her companionship after Alice's death. He feels, late in the book, some slight attraction to
Mick as she develops into adolescence. Generally, however, protective and kindly behavior toward women has replaced whatever sexual pleasure he enjoyed with a few prostitutes in a distant past. After Alice's sudden death, he expresses what might seem to be an unconventional "feminine" aspect of his personality as he sews and
begins to use Alice's perfume. At the same time, with monklike
austerity, he removes all the "feminine frills" from the apartment.
The narrator never states that Biff has had homosexual experience,
although he apparently has latent homosexual elements in his personality.

The vague and somewhat paradoxical aspects of Biff's personality
suggest that he is unable to integrate conflicting impulses. If he is a
"lonely hunter," he formulates his questions too vaguely to be able
to find convincing answers. Perhaps the most thoughtful
philosophical connection Biff makes occurs one morning as Alice
memorizes the text for her Sunday School lesson: "All men seek for
Thee." The verse briefly reminds him of his mother's religiosity,
but he also uses it to soften Alice's demand that he evict Jake
Blount, whom Biff has befriended, in a routine and emotionless
way. The validity of a search for truth through religion is never
emphasized in any of McCullers' work. But the human being locked
in his solitariness seeks always more than can be found. If he seems
to apprehend peace in human love or in relationship to a god, the
hope exists only in his imagination and the satisfaction is momentary.

The dream Singer has toward the end of the book suggests that it
may be interpreted as religious vision. In it, Spiros Antonapoulos

stands near the top of a stairs, Singer reaches up toward him, and Mick Kelly, Biff Brannon, Jake Blount, and Benedict Copeland, in turn, look up toward Singer. Antonapoulos holds an unrecognizable object. But the symbolism is so indefinite that the passage is baffling. Perhaps it implies that no clear answers to elemental questions exist. The sequence underlines the confusion and futility of human search for truth. Irony exists where the Divine Presence is one who cannot speak to those who reach up to him. That man creates god in his own image is ironically emphasized in this situation where a mute human being envisions a mute god. Even further irony lies in the fact that all are reaching up for wisdom from a man who himself reaches up to a mentally deficient being. Perhaps McCullers saw this as the extreme revelation that God must exist in many forms to answer the needs of so many "lonely hunters," who apparently have among themselves little sense of communion.

If in the dream Biff appears to recognize the need for religious experience to integrate human experience, and if he momentarily on one Sunday morning links a Bible verse to his memory of his mother, certainly McCullers does not follow this line of thought in revealing his character in the rest of the novel. His contact with others remains objective, orderly, and routinely scheduled. He tends to think only of the single day that he is living, and he never allows his identity to become deeply entangled with the lives of others as a result of recognizing a common element in their search for a god. His cafe, however, does provide a place where—as in *The Ballad of the Sad Cafe*—people are treated as if they have worth, even though they are freakish. Though little true fellowship is found in the cafe, the seekers do, in a sense, break bread together and the cafe is open both day and night for the lonely hunters.

The second member of the quartet, Jake Blount, twenty-nine, is confused in his socialist commitment. His plans for action are elaborated upon most vociferously when he is drunk. Always he claims the center of the stage. He will fight to defend a social reform until he is knocked unconscious, though neither he nor the workingman with whom he quarrels understands the theory over which they fight. A worker's resistance to, or fear of, revolt baffles Jake, because he assumes a worker deliberately rejects his salvation in rejecting active social protest. Jake clumsily demonstrates his interest in securing justice for black people when he blatantly patronizes the third member of the quartet, Dr. Benedict Mady Copeland. Jake embarrasses and offends the dignified, fifty-one-

year-old physician. Neither fully recognizes the other as a fellow
reformer. Copeland's Marxism is so highly intellectualized that he
communicates his theory no more effectively than does Jake in his
drunken rambling. By his harshness and inflexibility, Dr. Copeland
has long since driven away his wife and four children. He trusts
Singer as a kindly white person, but his companionship with him
tends to be superficial. Early in the book, on a hot night he sits, cold
and shaking with fever, in his darkened house. His daughter, Portia,
tries to draw him closer to herself, to his family, and to other black
people. Portia, Willie, and Portia's husband, Highboy, are at that
point a happy trio living together, sharing expenses, and enjoying
weekly Saturday night outings. Because they accept the position
society unfairly assigns them, Willie and Highboy hesitate even to
enter Dr. Copeland's house because he ridicules them, with their
compliant behavior, as "Uncle Toms."

Willie's harmonica music always signals his presence, but it is a
remote presence. Willie is arrested one night and prison guards
allow him and two other prisoners to suffer in such a cold cell that
their feet freeze and require amputation. After his tragedy, the harmonica is silent. His father takes him in and bitterly seeks
vengeance for his son's maltreatment. But when Jake tries to
publicize the tragedy as a dramatic example of capitalist oppression,
Willie is too frightened to cooperate, and Dr. Copeland is indignant
at what he considers the exploitation of Willie's misfortune.
Copeland feels revulsion that his son should be an object of pity. Instead, he wants all blacks to become proud, educated, strong—to
demand their rights.

Mick Kelly, with her rebellious and courageous spirit as she
moves from childhood into adolescence, dominates Part III of the
novel. While John Singer provides the structural center for the
book, McCullers knew—even when she had completed only Part I
and wrote her proposal to her publishers—that Mick, rather than
Singer, might seem to some readers the principal character, one of
the "heroic, though ordinary" figures to whom McCullers referred
in her initial outline of *The Mute*. Throughout the book, Mick's
pursuit of music symbolizes both her energy and her love of beauty.
She listens to concerts on the radios of families who happen to leave
their windows open, and later on she listens to the radio Singer buys
for his friends' pleasure. This music she stores in the "inner room"
of her personality into which she allows only Singer to enter. The
mundane she keeps at a safe distance from her inmost self in what

she conceives as her "outer room." Mick's plans to build her own violin from an old mandolin, for example, arise in her "inner room." Consequently, the frustration which accompanies failure in this project is far more bitter and violent than if the idea had grown in her "outer room."

Fortunately, her sexual initiation, when she bicycles into the country with Harry Minowitz, her shy neighborhood friend, merely baffles her in its suddenness and brevity, rather than producing psychic trauma. The impact of the experience is even more completely wiped out of her memory by greater violence when she returns home to discuss the event with Singer and discovers him dead. Harry, on the other hand, is shocked that he has violated a virgin— and has been himself defiled by contact with a gentile. He goes to another city to take a job there.

McCullers emphasized in her outline of the novel that she must deal with this sexual initiation lightly and with "extreme reticence."[2] It is clear that she did not want to convert Mick into a sexually sophisticated adult, nor did she wish to give either Mick or Harry any sense of either one's having found true love. The exuberant Mick, who savors life fully when she opens the door dividing her inner room from the outer room, is not to be found at the moment she loses her virginity. One sees her at her most vital moment when she climbs to the roof peak of an unfinished house and sits astride it, singing to the whole world.

Mick is ultimately a positively conceived character, though she also reveals many complicating limitations. At her worst, Mick cruelly taunts Bubber, her younger brother, the night he hides in a tree after he has accidentally shot "Baby" Wilson in the head. She tells him the police are searching for him, though she knows "Baby" is only superficially hurt and that it is only the hospital bill about which her parents must now worry. After the experience, Bubber is never again trusting, easily affectionate, and lighthearted. The change in him echoes the inhibiting and deadening one which takes place in Willie Copeland after his feet are amputated. Too late, Mick yearns for her little brother's companionship and for the loyalty she has destroyed in the one playmate she could count on to admire her.

At her best, Mick is heroic in offering to quit high school to support her family by working in the dime store—especially since this decision means she can no longer teach herself to play the piano in the school gym. Her defiant final words, "O.K. Some good!" show that she is still above despair and that she will battle the society that demands of her so unfair a sacrifice. Her inner world remains intact. She refuses to give up her ongoing sense that a meaningful pattern underlies the bitterness of her recent experiences.

Isolated, Mick fantasizes limitlessly to escape her parents' crowded boarding house. She possessively clings to privacy, symbolized by the assortment of treasures she keeps in a box under the bed in the room she must share with her disagreeable older sisters. She leaves unfinished her song, "This Thing I Want, I Know Not What," but she energetically moves through exciting visions of herself as celebrated composer, traveler, and inventor. If Singer's death unnerves her and she is bitter about giving up her piano lessons and school, this anger in itself reinforces the rebelliousness which will enable her to defy the fatality that overcomes her.

III   The Use of Black Characters

When *The Heart Is a Lonely Hunter* appeared in 1940, Richard Wright, whose *Native Son* also appeared that year, declared that the "most impressive aspect" of the book was "the astonishing humanity that enables a white writer, for the first time in Southern fiction, to handle Negro characters with as much ease and justice as those of her own race."[3] In his comment Wright might have been thinking of both Portia and Dr. Copeland. Portia strongly expresses her emotions and strongly revolts against isolation—particularly of one black from other blacks. Dr. Copeland expresses anger at the failure of blacks to demand their rights and, to some degree, accepts isolation from his own race as well as from whites as a political gesture.

Unlike her father, whose intellectual commitment to socialism destroys his close personal relationships, Portia expresses genuine feeling toward all of her associates. Fluently and gently, she expresses her affection for her father, but repeatedly she chides him for his moroseness and self-pity. She loves him freely—in spite of what he is, rather than because of what he is. She also surrounds with her secure love her insecure husband, Highboy, and her vulnerable brother, Willie. Portia mothers all of the Kelly children at the boarding house where she cooks and anxiously but submissively waits for her wages when the Kelly family is low on money. Her anger flares only in her anguished question: Why did Willie let a "no good" black woman get him into trouble?

To Portia, a reunion of the whole family at her grandfather's acreage would represent the ideal experience. The closest she comes to such harmony is in the careful management of a household to which she, Highboy, and Willie contribute equally; all of them look forward to the joys of Saturday nights together. At the close of the book, Willie is frightened and crippled by his prison experience, and Dr. Copeland, half-dead of tuberculosis, is carried in a farm wagon to spend his last days on the acreage which represents to Portia an idyllic haven but which represents to him the Negro's unnecessary and docile acceptance of rural poverty.

IV   A "*Contrapuntal*" Novel

At the time she outlined her book, McCullers assumed that John Singer, to whom the other four main characters would relate, would perplex them until his suicide at the end of Part II. At the point of Singer's death, however, they would begin to understand him, and, by extension, they would begin to understand themselves and each other. Actually, however, Singer's death baffles the characters more than did his life. Because his life was mysterious, its blurred outlines had allowed each person to create or define Singer as they wished him to exist. His suicide harmonized with no one's previous conception of him. No one knew the single-mindedness of his love for Antonapoulos or his longing for understanding. Singer, locked into his world of silence, actually is a static character; he does not respond to the other characters, whom he regards with eyes "cold and gentle as a cat's." He remains remote from them and simple in his daily life and in his love for one man. Only through their romantic creation of him, does Singer gain dramatic complexity. Because his suicide does not enhance the understanding of the four individuals or draw them together in community, the integration of themes for a dramatic finale cannot occur as McCullers had outlined it. Each experiences his bewilderment and grief alone.

McCullers again used musical terms to describe the style of her projected book as "contrapuntal throughout." Each character, she said, would be a voice in a fugue—a voice complete in itself but also enriched by contrast with the voices of other characters and by the subtle interweaving of his voice with the voices of the others. The contrapuntal effect would arise, she assumed, from her effort to establish a distinct style for each of the four characters who sought Singer's support. A fifth style, possessing the tone of a legend and the simplicity of a parable, she would use in presenting Singer. The differences in dialogue, pace, and tone which she achieves in the treatment of her five principal characters is remarkable. Because the style used for each character would subtly reflect his or her "inner psychic rhythm," McCullers thought it unnecessary for her to delve more explicitly into the "unconscious" of each character. Thoughts and feelings are revealed almost entirely through explicit action and direct dialogue. Relatively little reference is made to the past of each character, since it only minimally informs or determines his or her present behavior and thought. The narrator divulges only enough of the history of Biff Brannon and Dr. Copeland to intensify the impression of their present isolation. Almost nothing of the past lives of Mick Kelly, Jake Blount, or John Singer enters the novel.

Singer's total deafness suggests a pervasive silence which sets off every conversation and movement and contrasts with whatever noisy or violent action occurs, such as the street fights Jake Blount gets involved in or the riot at the carnival after the symbolic silence of Singer's death has entered the novel. This portrayal of silence is difficult for most authors. Perhaps McCullers' ability to make the reader "hear silence" arose from the sensitivity to sound which she gained from long musical training and from her habitual listening to recorded music whenever she wrote.

V   The Sense of Violence Held Tenuously in Check

Apart from its allegorical implications, the novel succeeds simply in terms of realistic narrative. Humor occasionally adds to the effect, particularly in Mick Kelly's tough arguments with the world. The sordid dullness of the town seldom rises to the surface of the reader's consciousness, but when it does, it reinforces the oppressive monotony of the lives of the characters. The monotony of the quiet lives of the characters contrasts with a number of episodes of violence which subtly build to cumulative effects.

In her book *Violence in Recent Southern Fiction*, Louise Gossett suggests that McCullers, even more than most contemporary Southern writers, portrayed with effectiveness that kind of violence which brings a "sickening sweep into the oblivion of complete isolation."[4] In *The Heart Is a Lonely Hunter* the accidental shooting of Baby Wilson by Bubber Kelly is superseded by the greater violence of Mick Kelly's taunting Bubber about the punishment he will receive in the electric chair, after she has found the little boy hiding in a tree in the dark. While Mick in her "inner room" dreams of beautiful music, she energetically paints and cherishes pictures of plane crashes, fires, and destructive storms. She is perversely ecstatic when her carefully planned formal party breaks up into a debacle as the guests chase one another across yards in the dark. The amputation of Willie Copeland's feet in prison is followed by the greater violence of Dr. Copeland's reaction not only to the brutality of the white prison guards but also to the gentle black people who, like his own wife and children, have accepted their suffering and oppression rather than fighting against it. Jake Blount's drunken fights and his beating in the carnival riot that makes him leave town are, McCullers suggests, a prelude to further violence. The shock of Antonapoulos's death leads to the greater violence of Singer's suicide as he grieves for his only companion. The shock reverberates in the lives of the four people who have surrounded Singer with their trust.

Perhaps most violent of all is the schism within the personality of Biff Brannon, who finds himself at the close of the novel suspended between male and female identification and between the past and the future and possessing little understanding of himself and of the present moment. Yet Biff appears to be, through routine discipline of himself and his daily schedule, in perfect control of a highly organized existence. The control of violence seems so tenuous in the lives depicted in this novel that McCullers communicates the terror that Flannery O'Connor once referred to as the slight "sense of suffocation" one feels upon awakening at the edge of a nightmare.

While *The Heart Is a Lonely Hunter* may not be McCullers' greatest work, it was a strong enough first novel to establish her in the very forefront of young American artists. It is essential to an understanding of the themes and techniques she was to develop more fully in her later work.

CHAPTER 3

Reflections in a Golden Eye *(1940)*

I *"An Army Post in Peacetime Is a Dull Place"*

CARSON McCullers produced *Reflections in a Golden Eye* in about two months, immediately after she completed *The Heart Is a Lonely Hunter.* She later recounted that, when she wrote this novel, she did not intend to publish it; but with the success of her first book in the summer of 1940, she quickly revised the second at Bread Loaf and arranged for it to appear in *Harpers Bazaar* in October and November 1940, with a dedication to her new friend Annemarie Clarac-Schwarzenbach. Book publication followed in February 1941. Many reviewers were strongly negative because of the novel's shocking subject matter; but nearly all of them, whether positive or negative, noted the great differences between her first two novels. Eventually, critics of this second novel discovered the remarkable tautness of McCullers' organization, the allegorical implications in the obsessive behavior of the characters, the impressive vision of evil that overshadows the work, and the macabre comedy that flashes through it.[1] In an overview of her work, the differences between her first and her second novels suggest her versatility and energy, qualities that insured her swift development in a tragically short career and that kept her from merely repeating her first novel. One can hardly imagine McCullers moving from *The Heart Is a Lonely Hunter* to the exploration of the demonic in *The Ballad of the Sad Cafe* without this portrayal of evil in a small, closed world as an intermediate step.

In *Reflections in a Golden Eye* McCullers explores, through the behavior of six characters, the violent, unusual, and unpredictable aspects of human behavior, which social convention and the uniformity quite often imposed by a military existence can almost

44

obscure. The geographic and social limits of a Southern army base circumscribe the action and lend a semblance of unity to otherwise chaotic and unpredictable situations. In this book McCullers depicts the cowardice, indulgence, perversion, cruelty, and self-hatred which one can associate with explicit portrayals of the seven deadly sins in medieval art; it has, in fact, been called "a modern morality play."[2] From the first pages, she suggests her principal theme: the contrast between the rigid discipline and monotony of the military establishment as opposed to the uncontrollable natural universe and to the permissive and egocentric behavior of the people who live on the base. Artificially imposed order and social conventions count for little in a comprehensive perspective of nature; they offer inadequate discipline for the uncontrolled and egocentric individual; and they may limit the development, revelation, and understanding of the complex human psyche.

The first section of *Reflections in a Golden Eye* presents the emotionless, and almost voiceless, Private Ellgee Williams, a country youth who instinctively loves sunshine, plants, and animals. He relates easily to the horses for which he cares, but remains remote from people, even from those with whom he works, eats, and sleeps. From the age of eight, he has avoided looking at women, because he has been taught that they carry a disease which makes men blind, deaf, and crippled—and may ultimately send them to hell. In his initial encounter with Ellgee, the rigid Captain Wendell Penderton reacts with great animosity toward this child of nature. Penderton's angry confrontation with the stolid and seemingly uncomprehending young man in the first pages of the book adumbrates their more violent encounter at its close. Typical of the stratified social life of the army, the Penderton cocktail parties include only officers and their wives, all of whom follow stilted patterns, even in their conversation. Their stultifying talk consists of little more than witticisms at the expense of others. In order to enlarge the view for guests at such parties, Penderton has ordered Williams to trim the trees and shrubs around his home, but has instructed him as to the exact limits within which he can cut back the lush growth. Williams, who knows nothing about Penderton's mania to compel living things to follow prescribed patterns, cuts away too much of the overgrowth, and exposes the Penderton house to plain view, a matter of consequence later in the action.

In this opening incident, McCullers introduces a second conflict, a hostile relationship between Penderton and his wife, Leonora. Their cold contempt for each other, however, escalates little throughout the book, because Leonora is too lazy and indifferent to all other people to stay angry and because Penderton knows her beauty adds to his social status. He wishes to retain her as an object and also to shelter himself from the speculation of others about his sexuality. Psychologically bisexual and physically impotent, he furtively seeks out fetishes—all of which are related to his penchant for cruelty or cleptomania. He is also perversely attracted to men who, like Colonel Morris Langdon or Private Williams, find his wife attractive.

Constant contention and ridicule characterize the relationship between the Pendertons. Leonora pointedly taunts Penderton as she observes the bewildered Williams in the opening scene: "The Captain wants you to pick up the branches and sew them back on again" (506).[3] Leonora, a strong, athletic woman, relaxes after riding as she watches her furious husband. She rocks in her hammock, drinking rye whiskey straight and washing it down with a single swallow of cold water. Penderton's anger intensifies as he commands her to change her clothes before the arrival of guests, who will include her lover, Major Morris Langdon. As rejoinder, Leonora, with quiet contempt, strips in the middle of the living room. Flaunting her nakedness, she strolls deliberately past the open door and up the stairs. The captain mutters threats of murder as she drawls, insolently looking down at him, "Son, have you ever been collared and dragged out in the street and thrashed by a naked woman?" (511) Meanwhile, outside the window, Ellgee Williams stares, as in a trance, at the nude figure.

Part II encompasses an incremental elaboration of the characteristics and history of each main figure in the novel: Captain Wendell Penderton and his wife, Leonora; Major Morris Langdon and his invalid wife, Alison; Alison's Filipino servant, Anacleto; and Private Ellgee Williams. But the principal figure in the action is Private Williams, who for twelve nights stealthily peers through the windows at Leonora and then begins each midnight to enter her room and squat motionless until almost dawn, watching her sleep. Such hypnotic fascination is not new to Ellgee; he has been accustomed to sit before the mess hall daily for an hour and simply stare as the wind ruffles two long lines of trees.

In Part III, Penderton's frustrated demand for authority breaks into violence. He attempts to force Leonora's uncontrollable horse, Firebird, to respond to his whimsical command, but finds himself, instead, carried wildly through the forest to what he thinks will be his death. When the horse finally halts, Penderton is enraged that the animal has proved as spirited and disobedient as Leonora herself and beats it brutally. The suffering horse seems near death as Penderton, lying exhausted on the ground, "like a broken doll" (552), gazes on Williams, who is coincidentally nearby, sunbathing behind a screen of undergrowth.

The unstable, abrasive spirit, which throughout the book lies barely controlled beneath the military protocol and the polite party conversation, breaks out clearly in the contentious remarks made by arrogant officers about Anacleto, who is this evening helping at the Penderton party. A dwarfed eunuch, Anacleto slavishly devotes himself to Alison, but, in brief episodes dispersed throughout Part III, he ridiculously indulges his vanity and his vindictiveness toward everyone except Alison. Like a nervous child, he is easily frightened or agitated, and his daydreams about a future alone with Alison are juvenile fantasies. The officers, mocking his accent, his infatuation, and his effeminate manner, raucously declare that a tough term in the military would "make a man" of him. Alison's husband feels contempt, rather than jealousy, for Anacleto. Derisively watching Anacleto dance down the stairs like a very dainty ballerina, Langdon is gratified when Anacleto trips himself and falls.

Much of the action of Part IV occurs, symbolically, in darkness. Penderton continues to follow Williams, hypnotically fascinated by the youth's freshness and beauty. Though he has previously considered enlisted men as a subspecies, he now envies them. He stares compulsively into the lighted windows of the barracks at sunset, longing for contact with Williams, who both attracts and angers him.

Neurotic and jealous of Leonora, who has replaced her as her husband's sexual partner, Alison is responsible, to a degree, for the violence which follows. One night, frightened by a premonition that she is dying, she observes a shadowy figure enter the Penderton house. She assumes hastily that the figure must be that of her husband and is especially indignant that he would visit Leonora's bedroom when Penderton is home. In her anger, she trails the intruder to the room, where, of course, she discovers him to be Williams. Although she rushes in consternation to Penderton, he refuses even to investigate her "hysterical report." He cannot envision the possibility that his stupid wife, Leonora, could be imaginative enough to deceive her lover, Morris Langdon, his comrade and superior officer.

The concluding events are, if anything, more bizarre. Later that night, after Alison announces her plans to file for divorce and to leave with Anacleto, Langdon precipitously arranges her commitment to a distant mental hospital, where she dies of a heart attack a day or two later. Anacleto disappears from the tale—possibly because there is no longer any Alison for him to devote himself to. Langdon grieves extravagantly for the wife he had consistently rejected. Some nights later, Penderton finally encounters Williams in Leonora's room and shoots him. As with the beating of the beautiful horse, Penderton again destroys more than he had intended. In death, Williams looks natural, innocent, and at peace, his suntanned palms turned upward. Penderton, on the other hand, now recognizing the dead man as the young soldier he had followed for several months, stands over the body like "a broken and dissipated monk" (594). Sleepy and bewildered, Leonora remains in her small world, where her mind and heart will never develop. That Williams is now dead hardly disturbs her.

II   *McCullers and the Gothic Mode*

Rather than juxtaposing positive and negative forces in conflict, McCullers in a consistently maintained vision illustrates the effects of essentially negative forces in this novel upon all the characters and all the situations. Her comic effects arise from the sudden introduction of startling detail, from the use of ironic contrast, or from the whimsical or deviant behavior of a character—outrageous behavior which she coolly implies may, after all, be commonplace. McCullers thus uses an incongruously casual tone to express grief or a mere parenthetical comment to convey some unspeakable horror. The catalogs or lists which she uses become comic by virtue of their exaggerated specificity or their mixing of significant with trivial items. Dramatic fusion of the horrible with the ridiculous produces a pervasive sense of distortion in the work, but the humorous effect is harsh rather than genial. Her objectivity in the narrative passages and in the descriptions of behavior precludes a full degree of empathy with any of the characters. The resulting detachment sometimes allows even distressing and bizarre situations to be viewed as dark comedy, much as if the action were happening to puppets instead of human beings. In *The Heart Is a Lonely Hunter*, because of McCullers' compassionate tone, the comic effects are only incidental, and we ultimately identify with her eccentric creations in their bizarre situations. It is only in this second book that she begins to experiment deliberately with techniques whose intended effects are comic, in spite of the disturbing nature of the cruelty, abnormality, and violence in her subject matter.

In this book no admirable figure, like Portia Copeland in the first novel, provides a touchstone for moral judgment or even a point of relief from the exaggerated and the grotesque. In the mundane world of the army post, boredom, self-centeredness, and futility imprison all of the characters, and only a few are capable of deep grief and despair. Violence, though frequently present, does not elevate the action toward tragedy, because the lives of these people seem of so little value to themselves or to others, and because the characters fail to respond to a crisis with the grief, fear, or revulsion that people usually reveal in such violent situations. In fact, only Alison Langdon in her care for her doomed baby rises above egocentricity for more than a moment. Internal conflict in the characters scarcely exists, because they are incapable of experiencing it.

Certain overtly dramatic scenes are memorable, but these sequences remain unconnected with others, as if to suggest the impossibility of strong relationships among the characters in the absence of rational pattern in the cosmos. The impact of these scenes, moreover, is not cumulative. Such intensity as exists inheres in the individual scene, and dramatic impact, for the most part, yields to an oppressive atmosphere as summer moves into autumn. The rows of identical buildings, as well as the routine life at the army base, reflect not only the monotony characteristic of life in a military compound but also the deadened sensibilities of army people themselves, who enjoy in peacetime a "surfeit of leisure and safety" (502). Because war characteristically connotes deliberate devastation, one might assume that the installation which trains soldiers for conflict would here provide an ominous setting for a work of fiction which moves toward a destructive confrontation between two army men. Though the novel moves toward destruction, it does so haphazardly and indirectly, so that the setting only remotely suggests impending violence. More immediately, the dehumanized military post suggests the utter aimlessness and futility of life in general, for people who have lost touch with values of any kind. Military activity in peacetime simply appears to be a game without point, whose players are complacent, enervated, maladjusted, or decadent. The patterned movements have no relationship to human affairs of consequence which, if they exist, lie beyond the limits of the army compound. In its violent incidents, grotesque characters, and acerbic humor, this tale might, then, be interpreted as a satire upon the military ethos at its worst—conformist, hierarchical, hedonistic, and complacent. The chaotic nature of the book even suggests the possibility that no fixed norms or common values exist.

Carson McCullers, however, chose never to defend this stark novel on metaphysical grounds. In fact, she pointedly disregarded in her discussion of it the philosophical overtones which it unmistakably does possess. When critics decried its morbidity or perversity, she countered that they should not impose upon fantasy the criteria appropriate to the interpretation of realistic fiction. Similarly, when reviewers contrasted unfavorably its one-dimensional characters with the complex figures of her first novel, she maintained that neither convincing motivation nor subtle portrayal were appropriate for a fairy tale. When the book was still in galleys, she defended in talks with other writers at Bread Loaf its sensational qualities and its melodramatic effects by insisting that her characters and situations were to be laughed at, since they are part of a world which she had envisioned as stylized, exaggerated, grotesque, and grimly humorous.[4] One recognizes even more clearly such stylization in her next book, *The Ballad of the Sad Cafe*. In both books, she was more interested in the bald incongruities reflected in the interactions of her characters than in exploring the psychic origin of behavior that most readers would regard as abnormal. Nevertheless, though McCullers denied that she had expressed any serious satirical intent in *Reflections in a Golden Eye*, the book reflects, in its celebration of irrational behavior, her profound distrust of the intelligence as an exclusive means for interpreting human experience and her growing distrust of realism as a literary mode which relies upon rationally stated motivations for its characters.

If Carson saw her book as a comic fairy tale, early reviewers labeled it "Southern gothic." Some irony exists in the fact that she published about this time her first critical article, in which she objected to the overuse of the term "Southern gothic" in studies of current fiction emanating from the South.[5] Although she considered the dominant trend in Southern writing to be realistic and saw gothicism as highly romantic and idiosyncratic, and although she had written her first novel in a realistic mode, she turned in *Reflections in a Golden Eye*—and again in *The Ballad of the Sad*

Cafe—to experimentation with those nonrealistic literary conventions often regarded as "gothic." In her essay she never denied the effectiveness of gothic fiction; she only questioned whether it had become the prevalent genre in the South that critics of Southern literature suggested.

As early as 1937, she had recognized a kinship with Isak Dinesen (Karen Blixen) in her enjoyment of the Danish writer's graphic and autobiographical *Out of Africa* and her *Seven Gothic Tales*. All the rest of her life she ritualistically reread Dinesen each year, and Dinesen's fiction provided her with her strongest influence for experimentation with the gothic mode. Dinesen's ability to unite comedy with horror and her ability to combine the realistic with the fantastic are remarkable. McCullers' first critical essay on Dinesen appeared in 1943 when she reviewed *Winter's Tales*. Certainly by the time McCullers finished *Reflections in a Golden Eye* in the summer of 1940, she had assimilated into her own fiction the elements customarily associated with the gothic mode: its combination of the violent and comic, and its abrogation of the world of the rational. In spite of McCullers' documentation of routine military life in *Reflections in a Golden Eye*, she had gone far beyond satirical realism in her preoccupation with irrational behavior, in her focus upon the intuitive and sensual, and in her emphasis on natural landscape and animals as symbols of the uninhibited, unconscious elements in the psyche.

III   The Fragmented Vision of Human Existence

The behavior of all of the characters in this novel is erratic, reflecting their incomplete, distorted, and inconsistent attitude toward life. The inconsistencies, characterizing their actions, result in a book that is difficult to explicate fully. The movement, often occurring through metaphor, remains elusive. The images frequently are inconsecutive and suggest the disoriented vision from which the book originates. Among the dominant symbolic images to be found in the book are fierce or many-faceted eyes; distorting mirrors; shimmering or strangely colored sunlight; changing patterns of shadows, clouds, and stars; brilliant flashes of light; and the blur of rapidly moving objects or changing landscapes. Horror and ugliness result from McCullers' vision in this book, but so do serenity and beauty. Reality, as perceived by the characters in this

novel, is fragmented, blurred, and out of proportion—like the grotesque reflections to be found in the golden eye of a jeweled peacock.

For example, more dramatic in its artistic impact than Penderton's beating of Firebird is his heightened sensory perception and loss of perspective in the wild ride which precedes the episode. Having reached the point of absolute terror and having relinquished all hope of survival, he suddenly becomes exultant as death seems certain. Though he is characteristically a bullying officer, he now abandons himself to the peculiarly pleasurable pain of submissiveness and powerlessness as the horse catapults him through space. With remarkable control of imagery based on smells, tactile sensations, warmth and cold, sounds and silence, and stark visual perceptions, McCullers exploits Penderton's ambivalent emotions, his simultaneous terror and exhilaration. As the horse races through the trees, tearing Penderton's skin on pine cones and branches, the captain loses his sense of proportion and perspective. Forced to cling sideways on the horse, he watches from a peculiar angle as the world sweeps past too rapidly for him to perceive objects separately.

Despite this blurring of his sight, he responds to nature at this moment more sensitively and sensuously than he ever had before. He is aware now that the afternoon is sunny and that the air is "bracing, bittersweet with the odor of pines and rotting leaves" (549). As if delirious, he experiences an intensity he has never felt before, and he now also begins to apprehend nature with the rapture that a mystic might reveal. The world becomes kaleidoscopic— a white flower in the dead leaves glows incandescently, a thorny pine cone streaks the blood of his cheek across his eyes, a bird flies in the windy sky, and suddenly there appears "a fiery shaft of sunshine in the green gloom" (551).

This disturbance of the captain's senses, which culminates in the beating of Firebird, recurs again late in the book just before Penderton murders Williams. Penderton's senses again run away with him and he becomes hypersensitive. Because of his growing attraction toward Williams and his simultaneous hatred of him, he one day dismisses a class in great agitation, when he realizes that he no longer knows which soldiers are seated before him or what words to speak to them. Another day he witnesses the collision of a car and truck, but the crash impresses him exactly as much as the newspaper fluttering by in the wind a moment later. Preternatural awareness of the weather, experienced simultaneously by Penderton and Williams, determines, in part, the psychological drama of the last day of Williams' life. Like an animal sensing danger, Williams feels that a storm is about to break and he runs for shelter, while Penderton, paralyzed by indecision and frustration, is drenched by the bitterly cold November rain. That night Penderton hears a sound outside; for one second he sees Williams revealed by the match struck in the darkness at the edge of the woods where he had slipped in the mud from the afternoon rain. Moments later, Penderton stands over the body of the man he has killed in Leonora's room and recognizes that it is Williams.

Although she carefully documents the regimented aspects of military life, McCullers in this novel actually creates a universe without fundamental order or direction, and the values reflected in the action throughout the book are relative rather than representative. She reports carefully the details of obsessive behavior and of confused perception, but she explores only superficially the realm of the psyche. She does not enter the minds of the compulsive individuals, though she exploits for dramatic and literary effect the bizarre quality of their behavior. She avoids overt use of the supernatural, but she creates a distorted, macabre world as a result of the way in which her characters fearfully misinterpret the ordinary and the natural. For example, for Ellgee, time stands motionless as he waits beside Leonora's bed from midnight to dawn. The world stops turning until the sun's first rays appear. Whenever Penderton, Alison, and Anacleto are under stress, objects assume for them abnormal shapes. Proportions and dimensions enlarge or contract, and colors change. If the rows of barracks, the military regimen, and the cocktail party schedules never change, even this monotony breeds its own revulsion, as of a nightmare from which the characters would like to escape but by which they are imprisoned in moments of terror, perceived as suffocation. Langdon, Williams, and Leonora lack sensitivity and are generally imperturbable to events and people around them. Penderton, Alison, and Anacleto, with greater awareness of intellectual and emotional interaction, sometimes perceive the constricted world of the military base as a hell where one's vision can only be fragmented, blurred, and distorted. Because all behave from moment to moment as this nightmare world dictates, instincts and unreason dominate and moral direction or rational response seem impossible or irrelevant.

IV   The Primitive and Demonic: Echoes of D. H. Lawrence

Certain critics have suggested the influence of D. H. Lawrence on McCullers, since *Reflections in a Golden Eye* bears some notable similarities to "The Prussian Officer."[6] In both tales a frustrated and somewhat sadistic officer with unacknowledged homosexual propensities compensates for his impotence and jealousy by persecuting a country youth of lower military rank. In Lawrence's story the soldier finally rebels and kills the officer, although in both tales the young soldiers are long-suffering. In both, the free and open universe of nature contrasts with the constricted and rigid life in a military unit. In McCullers' tale, a lush forest reserve surrounds the army post; in Lawrence's story, snow-covered mountains envelop much of the action. In both tales, the murderer is himself figuratively destroyed by the violence he commits. At the end, Lawrence's soldier loses himself in spirit in the snowy landscape. Ironically, he is placed in death by the side of the officer. He achieves in death a sense of peace that had been lost to him once the officer noticed him. With a similar serenity, Williams welcomes death, as he turns his palms upward as if to capture the warmth of the sun.

Despite these similarities, the works differ significantly. Lawrence's story, unrelieved by McCullers' flashes of ironic comedy, is even more sinister than *Reflections in a Golden Eye*. It is, at first, less abrasive, since most of the characters restrain their emotions with some success until the climactic scene of violence. Except for the bewilderment and clumsiness of the peasant youth in the opening scenes, where Lawrence at first treats him with a degree of whimsicality, nothing in the tone, characterization, or situation in "The Prussian Officer" suggests that Lawrence saw his story as a humorous fairy tale, as McCullers insisted that she envisioned hers. Though Williams and, to a degree, Leonora Penderton and Morris Langdon, are close to the world of animal nature, a stronger sense of the force of the primitive suffuses Lawrence's tale.

Ellgee Williams' annoyance at being followed by Penderton is not extreme: he is, in fact, only as aware of Penderton's interest in him as he is aware of changes in the weather. He lacks the sense of being malignantly persecuted that plagues Lawrence's soldier. Penderton's tentative dogging of Williams provides no close parallel to the Prussian officer's sadism toward the youth, who must endure extended marches, go without sleep, and suffer kicks and bruises. Penderton focuses his cruelty less directly, though he gains satisfaction from maltreating Firebird and dropping a kitten into a mailbox to freeze to death. Ellgee Williams lacks the Prussian youth's remarkable endurance, his pride, and his stoical pretense that he feels no pain even after much physical and mental abuse. References to Ellgee Williams' half-forgotten murder of a Negro are only incidental and hardly suggest that Williams will kill Penderton.

Conversely, in Lawrence's story the tension mounts steadily to a strong crescendo, since his focus is on two characters only and on the potentially deadly conflict between them. Dramatic tension is lessened, perhaps intentionally, by the length of McCullers' narrative, which allows her to introduce several characters besides Penderton and Williams, to follow several threads of action, and to distract or edify the reader with touches of macabre humor. Certainly, the basic conflict between an officer and an enlisted man is similar in the two works, as are the unpredictable violence, the abuse of power, and the symbolic role of landscape. With his emphasis upon nature and upon the unnatural and his apprehension of the demonic in the psychic life, Lawrence exists somewhere in the background of McCullers' novel.

V Isolation as a Recurring Motif

As in *The Heart Is a Lonely Hunter*, each man and woman in *Reflections in a Golden Eye* exists in a state of spiritual isolation, induced largely by his or her own fears and fantasies. The result of such insecurity and imaginative extravagance is inevitable destruction when the self-indulgence or self-hatred surpasses the capabilities of the individual to control it. While the characters actually cross each other's paths on the post, they do not interact closely with one another until violence or fatality overpowers them. Penderton follows Williams at a distance or tries to gain a glimpse of him through the barracks windows. Williams and Leonora occupy the same small room each night, but she is absolutely unaware of his presence, as she is of the other people's feelings and thoughts when she is with them. No closeness exists in the two marriages, that of the Langdons nor that of the Pendertons. The actions of the characters exist in separate patterns, which hardly ever intersect, though all the people are confined to one tiny stage. If the world of the army post is narrow, each character lives within his own world, which is still more narrow. In this respect only, the book strongly resembles *The Heart Is a Lonely Hunter*. Significant communication between individuals, involving their minds and hearts, is totally absent, though McCullers' view of her characters is sympathetic to the extent that she would seem to deplore their constricted and barren existence.

Ellgee Williams possesses the same capability for the destruction of others and of himself that a natural force possesses. He moves with the silence of a shadow or the stealthiness of a nocturnal animal throughout the novel, never speaking more than a few syllables; reacting reflexively rather than purposefully; staring always as if in a hypnotic trance; and responding only to animals or to the sun, grass, and wind. If he possessed a sense of individual identity when he left the farm, he symbolically lost even that when he enlisted and had to give up his name, L.G. A sergeant yelled, "You can't go into the U.S. Army with a goddam name like that," and promptly christened him Ellgee (566).

If irrationality has destructive consequences, it sometimes furnishes a character like Ellgee with extraordinary insight. From the beginning, McCullers envisions him as possessing the wildness, deviousness, and lack of intelligence of an animal: "In his eyes. . .there was a mute expression that is found usually in the eyes of animals" (502). He has the mistrustfulness of an untamed animal, "a certain watchful innocence," and he moves "with the silence and agility of a wild creature or a thief" (503). Because his instinctual responses scarcely register in his conscious mind, he is unencumbered by guilt or responsibility. He is aware of having made only four decisions in his life—to buy a cow, to be saved in a Holiness meeting, to kill a man, and to enlist. In each case, only after he had acted on the decision did he seem to know that he had made it.

Williams' closeness to nature, though obvious, is never idealized. Because he lacks the reflective capacity to reach self-knowledge, he remains more brute than human. He is absolutely egocentric, never thinking of his effects on others. So completely does he avoid extremes of feeling that no one has seen him laugh, become angry, or suffer during the time that he has been in the army. Though he once murdered a man, his passive disposition belies such capacity for violence. Williams reveals an obsession, however, that will be fatal to him—a fascination with what he also most dreads—contact with a nude woman. He dimly realizes, however, that the female is a destructive force, even while he is drawn in a kind of trance to

Leonora each night. He does not truly see her; in fact, he scarcely recognizes her in the daytime when she is out of doors, vigorously athletic, riding her horse, and laughing mockingly at him. Though his experience in her bedroom is totally sensual, he never expresses sexuality overtly. His enjoyment lies in "the thick rug beneath his feet, the silk spread, the faint scent of perfume. . .the soft luxurious warmth of woman-flesh, the quiet darkness" (592), while he masturbatorily drifts with feelings that then surge through him.

A lover of the open clearings in the forest where the sun is hot against his naked body, he is not truly an open or outgoing individual, but almost as furtive and covert in his behavior as Penderton. In the latter part of the book he is more often lurking in darkness than enjoying the sun. If he finds rapport with animals, he remains always at a distance from the people whose lives he seems to monitor silently. He acknowledges Penderton's attention to his movements only as he passively accepts the landscape or the weather, not questioning Penderton's stalking of him "any more than he would question a thunderstorm or the fading of a flower" (591).

Ellgee scarcely remembers, moreover, the man he had killed five years before, a Negro with whom he argued over a wheelbarrow of manure. But he recalls the physical sensations surrounding the experience—the heat of the July afternoon, the color of blood, and the smell of dust as he dragged away the body. He does not identify himself conceptually as the murderer of a human being: "The mind of Private Williams was imbued with various colors of strange tones, but it was without delineation, void of form" (567). In short, he never becomes, for better or for worse, a truly developed human being capable of relating to other human beings or capable of forming even the most elementary moral discriminations.

Leonora, also uninhibited and living for satisfaction of physical appetite, remains as primitive in her behavior as Ellgee. Not silent like him, she is incapable of sustained thought. Totally sensual, she loves to ride, to exercise in the out of doors, to sleep naked, to drink with gusto, and to have a vigorous sexual life with whomever she wishes.

Captain Wendell Penderton lives for the expression of his sadistic and masochistic impulses; and they sometimes achieve expression in lurid visions. He takes Seconal to induce dreams of "truth" which are mirrored in the eye of a terrifying bird which enfolds him in its huge black wings. When he fixes his mind on something, Penderton often acts involuntarily, much like Williams, and such fixation of his mind or energies may cause him to engage in covert acts of stealing, beating, or killing. Immediately preceding and following such furtive acts, he feels omniscient and omnipotent, but achieves such satisfying self-expression only when he is alone with an object or creature in his power. If others observe him use that power, he feels that his extreme actions have, in turn, put him in their power. When he beats Firebird and Williams watches, or when he steals a spoon and Alison notes the act, he feels trapped and desolate rather than relieved and renewed.

Consistent with his military background, Penderton is committed to organization and discipline, and he seeks to control the living things in his immediate world by blatant self-assertion—he trims trees and shrubs that grow too freely, he quarrels with his wife, who is completely pleasure-loving, or he tortures kittens and horses, which live instinctively. Ironically, these attempts to control other living things lead to frustration and violence. The violence, in turn, often induces a still greater frustration and an eventual exhaustion and despair. His momentary assertions of power emphasize, in fact, his most negative aspects, his cowardice, his impotence, and his inhumanity. Even at the end, we know little of the forces that shaped this enigmatic and desperate man, except that five solicitous spinster aunts had had a dominating role in his upbringing.

Morris Langdon resembles Penderton in his commitment to a military career, but he is an imperturbable hedonist rather than a sado-masochist. Like Leonora and Ellgee Williams, Langdon is generally relaxed, tolerant, unintellectual, uncomplicated, and—on the surface—healthy and sensible. Unlike Penderton, he does not seek out visions to confirm his psychic tendencies. In fact, he lacks insight and sees only the most superficial aspects of the people who stand before him. While McCullers in this book is not interested in the exhaustive analysis of the psychic life, at times the very lack of any probing of her characters throws whatever contradictions they reveal into clearer light—for instance, Langdon's engaging simplicity in social situations where that contrasts with his insidious lack of sensitivity toward his wife. Forthright and sure of himself and his world, he has achieved already his own ambitions: "a healthy body and patriotism" (587). If such ambitions seem innocuous, McCullers also reveals in him the fact that a man of simplicity and grace may lack imagination and sympathy. For example, he listens a day and a half to his wife scream in childbirth. Then, because his daughter is born with a frail body and two fingers joined, he refuses ever to touch her in her eight months of life.

Anacleto is a shadowy figure who yet causes other characters to stand in a clearer light as they react to him. He prefigures the dwarf, Cousin Lymon, who acts as a similar catalyst in McCullers' next book, *The Ballad of the Sad Cafe*. Like Lymon, Anacleto is not clearly a male or female; he is ageless, though childlike in appearance; and he is an outsider in a tightly closed social group. As a romantic or sexual partner for Alison, he is as ineffectual as Lymon is for Miss Amelia. Both tiny men are seen talking long into the night with the lonely women to whom they attach themselves. Both disappear from the community when the women meet their doom.

Although Alison foolishly dreams of a romantic life with Anacleto, she is basically clear-sighted and often courageous. Looking into the golden, jeweled eye of the bird which Anacleto paints, she sees its fragmented facets as "grotesques," and she perceives the artifice which the bird represents as unwholesome, "a sort of ghastly green" (564). She is the only one who recognizes Ellgee Williams' expressionless face upon first glance as "a Gauguin primitive" (534), seeing in him a potentially positive and intuitive person, as well as a limited one. Her sharp vision causes her also to see Williams enter the Penderton house in the dark and later to report this incident accurately. Ironically, her perspicacity is deemed insanity by Penderton and by her husband, who cannot face the reality which she discloses to them.

If Alison is the most clear-sighted character, she is herself the subject of much persecution and has her significant limitations. Others see her, with much accuracy, as a big-nosed, white-faced, sickly woman. Penderton hates her, Leonora considers her to be an absurdly innocent child to whom she must always speak loudly and distinctly, and her husband simply ignores her. She refuses to become angry even when she has justification, and she lacks self-respect. When she learns, for instance, that her husband is unfaithful to her, she patiently knits a suit for his mistress, identifying closely with the woman who shares with her the attentions of an unworthy man. Of more consequence than her dream about a future with Anacleto or her grief about a past in which her child died after a few months, is her constant hatred of herself, which prevents her from ever seeing past, present, and future in perspective.

Though Alison is more sensitive and responsive than the rest of the people in her circle, she lacks strength to free herself from them because she cannot give expression to her own strength of character. When she cuts off her nipples with a garden shears in an exaggerated rite of self-abasement, her husband merely dismisses the incident, and the Pendertons regard it as an embarrassing secret known only by a doctor and a nurse. The act evokes no sympathy nor understanding.

Alison becomes strong and vital only near the end when she is alone and faces the premonition of her death. She confronts it at first with courage, forcing herself to remember her few independent years when life had had some meaning for her. Waking at two in the morning with the sudden understanding that she is soon to die (she does, in fact, die two days later), she sits up in bed and begins to knit. She recalls, detail by detail, her rigorous life as a schoolteacher in Vermont, where she lived happily with her cats and dogs, where she served herself hot chili, tea, and zwieback, and where she chopped her own wood. Suddenly, the beating (and perhaps breaking) of her heart becomes loud, monotonous, and unbearable, and she drops her knitting: "The room was silent as a sepulcher and she waited with her mouth open and her head twisted sideways on the pillow. She was terrified, but when she tried to call out and break this silence, no sound would come" (560).

Moments later, she realizes that Anacleto is holding her hand. But his presence does not allay her terrors, for she sees that his "sickly grimace" but mirrors her own expression. When Alison is unable to cry out for help, the scene is far more powerful than the violent, exaggerated, and melodramatic incidents in the book. Her silent death spasm, for example, eclipses, in its tragic implications, her act of self-mutilation.

Alison cannot endure the impersonal routine of the military compound, but she cannot reject its mundane rituals and realities, either. It is as if existence on the army post is unreal and a nightmare, hardly allowing one to adapt to any other sort of life. Like other characteristics in the book, Alison lacks the clarity of vision and the strength of will to alter the stultifying society of which she is part or to free herself from it.

VI   *McCullers' Versatile Artistry*

Though *Reflections in a Golden Eye* disappointed many critics who had so recently discovered Carson McCullers as a writer of great promise, this book reveals a technical virtuosity which, in some respects, surpasses that found in her first novel. For example, the methods by which McCullers achieved ironic humor in *The Ballad of the Sad Cafe* and *The Member of the Wedding* she first established in *Reflections in a Golden Eye*.

The use of a narrative voice marked by emotional detachment, formality, concision, and some artifice suggests an undeviating attitude of superiority, on the speaker's part, and his awareness of the absurdity of the characters and situations. While the narrative passages do not clearly specify a speaker who is a character in the book, like the storyteller in *The Ballad of the Sad Cafe,* who identifies himself as a worker at the textile mill down the road from the cafe, they do suggest the presence of a narrator whose views seem close to those of McCullers herself. As in her next two books, McCullers' passages of narrative include simplistic statements, comic exaggeration, excessive explicitness, and an emphasis upon tedious or mundane detail as well as upon dramatic and significant events. Her playful use of lists, characterized by minute detail or by the inclusion of a single inappropriate item in a series, becomes a notable comic device in her next two books. She also begins here her characteristic linking of three people, three objects, or three facts. Sometimes the lists or parallel sentences or phrases are soberly intoned and sound either like lines of poetry or like rhetorical flourishes.

McCullers suggests at some points the style of the teller of the tall-tale of frontier days as he convinces the reader, for example, of Williams' strange limitations. With much detailed evidence, the narrator establishes Williams' penchant for incomprehensible behavior and his utter stupidity. A leap in logic is then made: if Ellgee is like this, the whole human race may be even more foolish—at least that part of the human race which is in the United States Army. A passage follows which suggests that, despite his primitive naiveté, Ellgee may well be the most sensible soldier in his barracks:

One old Corporal wrote a letter every night to Shirley Temple, making it a sort of diary of all that he had done during the day and mailing it before breakfast the next morning. Another man, who had ten years' service behind him, jumped out of a three-story window because a friend would not lend him fifty cents for beer. A cook in the same battery was haunted by the fixed idea that he had cancer of the tongue, an illusion that no medical denials could dispel. He brooded before a mirror with his tongue out so far that he could see the taste-buds, and he starved himself to the point of emaciation. (591)

Another instance of McCullers' virtuosity occurs when she uses a series of three parallel grammatical elements to make Leonora's retardation laughable by stressing that it causes no pain—for herself, her father, her husband, or her lover. In fact, the three men of normal intelligence, it is implied, are less sensitive about the desirability or necessity for intelligence in a woman than even Leonora is:

The truth of the matter was that she was a little feeble-minded. . . . There were only three persons who understood this: her old father, the General, who had worried no little about it until she was safely married; her husband, who looked on it as a condition natural to all woman under forty; and Major Morris Langdon, who loved her for it all the more. (512)

McCullers sustains, furthermore, a tone of mockery by a stylistic terseness which reveals in a sentence or two or a short sequence the ridiculous, odd, or petty nature of the individual involved. The narrator reveals, in just such a pointed sequence, Anacleto's basic interest in trouble-making and malevolence toward others, which prevents him from becoming a saintly figure in his devotion to Alison. When one evening Anacleto wishes Leonora, Wendell, and Morris Langdon a pleasant good-bye, he hopes to see them fall where he has placed three bricks at the end of the front walk. When they unwittingly elude his scheme by cutting across the lawn, he is, like a frustrated urchin, "so vexed that he gave his thumb a mean little bite" (574). In this sequence he reveals himself as foolish and vindictive, a trouble-maker like Cousin Lymon in *The Ballad of the Sad Cafe*, not benevolent and sympathetic as we might expect him to be, given the purity of his feeling for Alison.

Alison herself is at times a foolish woman, although she is the most human character in the book. In the final glimpse of her, McCullers simply shows her and Anacleto staying awake until dawn looking at an atlas. They have announced that they are leaving to establish the good life in the promised land. Now they must decide where that land will exist. Before morning, they settle on a mere dot on the map—Moutreville, South Carolina—a decision involving mere caprice and little capacity to see their situation fully as it exists.

In another brief vignette, McCullers reveals her insight into the hypocrisies that underlie much conventional social behavior, when Leonora offers perfunctory consolation to the ailing Alison. With her usual stupidity, Leonora arrogantly assumes that she knows more than anyone else about the proprieties to be observed in a sick room. One should pretend to look ill, stay for one full hour, and avoid speaking of anything except illnesses. Alison is, thus, treated to an hour of Leonora's "good manners" as Leonora recounts, with painfully screwed-up face, all the stories she has ever heard of people who have fallen from horses and the complications of their recoveries or their failures to recover.

If growth in comic artistry is notable as a result of her use of detached narrative passages and her use of anecdotal glimpses into the oddity and meanness of her characters, other evidence of her artistic versatility is her use of landscape to suggest the passage of time or to intensify a mood or a situation. The brilliant sunny days of early autumn when Ellgee has not yet entered Leonora's room contrast with the later oppressive atmosphere when the action takes place at night and as cold rain and wind increase. Late in the book, night comes ominously when the sound of the bugle, magnified in the wind, is heard "echoing in the woods with a lost hollow tone" as the night envelops the land. The wind, blowing for two days without stopping, strips the maples of their leaves. The leaves then lie like a golden blanket while in the cold rain the bare branches of the trees become a filigree against the winter sky. On the final night of his life, chilled by the rain and covered with the mud he has fallen into, Williams has only the light and warmth of one match for one second. It is as if in such cold the soldier, who has always turned his palms upward to the sun, now reaches out his hands to death.

McCullers sometimes uses the impersonal phenomena of nature to contrast with the personal situations of her characters and to set them in a total perspective. She thus dramatizes the slow passage of time as Ellgee waits each night by Leonora's bed by describing the slight changes taking place in the night sky. He waits two hours at the edge of the forest after the last light in the house is out; he then waits for the stars to fade and for the night to turn to "deep violet," for Orion to become brilliant, and for the Big Dipper to shine with "wonderful radiance." Then as the sky becomes paler and as Venus fades, he hurries out of the house. Ellgee does nothing but stand motionless during these long hours when the only motions occurring in the book are the silent changes taking place in the sky. On the night of his death the silence becomes more oppressive in contrast to the loudness of the striking of his match, and the blackness of the night is made more intense by the brightness of this single flicker of light, which also alerts his murderer to his presence.

In her use of lurid experience and in her experimentation with stylized characters and narration, McCullers approaches in this book the gothic mode of which she had become so distrustful. *Reflections in a Golden Eye* thus represents a break with the realism informing *The Heart Is a Lonely Hunter* and adumbrates the imaginative fantasy and the psychological exploration of complex patterns of attraction and repulsion among human beings by means of stylized two-dimensional characters who seem not quite human in *The Ballad of the Sad Cafe*.

In other novels by McCullers, love has power to nurture or to destroy the solitary people it touches. In this novel, the characters play a mad game in which they only destroy each other and themselves; love does not truly exist, except in terms of self-gratification (though Anacleto and Alison are not exclusively so self-centered). Nothing really matters in the world projected in this book. The golden eye reflects the world of the characters as fragmentary, and the broken fragments of reality reflected in this golden eye are oppressive and not in any way reassuring. It is unclear whether McCullers implies that the cosmos is fundamentally askew or that the limitations of human beings themselves give rise to a society that has little continuity and meaning. She would seem to imply that if human beings could be more rational and selfless, the universe, if finally inexplicable, would, at least, become more bearable and hospitable to them.

If one cannot always respond to the fusion of horror and comedy and cannot always see the necessity of some macabre incidents, the carefully controlled structure, the precision and occasional beauty of the prose, and the tension of the last scenes cause one to see this book as more remarkable than its first readers recognized. As Louis Untermeyer wrote before it was published, it seems to proceed "from some inner compulsion . . . inevitable as life itself." If McCullers' talent had not yet found its full expression, this work was, as Untermeyer continued, "one of the most compelling, one of the most uncanny stories ever written in America."[7]

CHAPTER 4

The Ballad of the Sad Cafe *(1943)*

I N *The Ballad of the Sad Cafe* McCullers achieeved an intricate blending of the real and the mythic, of the comic and the
desolate, and of the provincial and the universal. She attained in
this short novel an extraordinary compression, control, objectivity,
and sense of proportion. The narrative voice speaks at times in
archaic diction and at times in a tone of leisured elegance; at still
other times, in a pithy colloquial idiom. Though the three principal
characters are grotesques, rather than fully-developed human beings and the villagers are not individualized, the "balladeer's" compassion for them pervades this book, as does his quiet humor when
he pauses in the narrative to comment upon their inexplicable, eccentric, and often perverse behavior.

I   A Turbulent Relationship

Kay Boyle declared *The Ballad of the Sad Cafe* a work in which
an author "accepted the responsibility of being artisan as well as
sensitive artist."[1] As in *Reflections in a Golden Eye*, McCullers attains in this novel an allegorical or "fairy-tale" exaggeration in her
characters. Their freakishness, Boyle suggests, moves them beyond
the range of ordinary human experience. Nevertheless, the thematic
content of *The Ballad of the Sad Cafe* is not so remote as Boyle in-
timates from McCullers' personal life, her search for self-
identification, and her exploration of unusual sexual experience. In
creating intricate emotional diversities as characteristic of the life of
Miss Amelia Evans, McCullers reflects, to a degree, the turbulence
of her own life at the time she wrote this work, a turbulence emerg-
ing from the compounding of deep conflicts and complex
relationships—the love and hate she felt for Reeves, whom she was
divorcing; the strong, but frustrated, love she felt for her new friend

Annemarie Clarac-Schwarzenbach; and the bewildering, but warm, affection she was discovering for David Diamond, who was attracted both to her and to Reeves. In *The Ballad of the Sad Cafe* McCullers assimilated all of these confused loves and disappointments when she conceived and almost completed the tale in the summer of 1941 at Yaddo and announced to Diamond that she would dedicate it to him.

The fact that *Reflections in a Golden Eye* was dedicated to Annemarie Clarac-Schwarzenbach in the summer of 1940 and *The Ballad of the Sad Cafe* to David Diamond the following summer suggests how fully McCullers had by this time confronted her bisexuality and that of her husband, who was during these months living with Diamond in New York. In this novel McCullers explores such themes as sexual ambivalence, destructive infatuation, the pain of being rejected by the beloved, the problematical configurations implied in any love triangle, and the paradoxical closeness of love and hate.

McCullers, hoping to return with renewed creativity to the uncompleted *The Bride* (later *The Member of the Wedding*), expected, for a time, to publish both of these short works in the same volume. However, the subtle balance of mood, theme, and image she sought in the story of Frankie Addams' adolescence continued to evade her until 1945. In the meantime, she published *The Ballad of the Sad Cafe* in *Harpers Bazaar*, August 1943.

Though Carson McCullers ostensibly used a southern mill town as setting for *The Ballad of the Sad Cafe*, the locale is also an imaginatively created milieu inhabited by grotesque and improbable characters—a milieu, for example, in which a female giant, Miss Amelia Evans, possesses, in the eyes of the villagers, awesome powers. As the tale opens and as it closes, life in the village is so static that "the soul rots with boredom" (65),[2] but for a short time between the opening of the story and its final sequence, the town becomes a place where strange and unbelievable events occur and where the three principal participants exist in some indefinable state between the human and the supernatural.

McCullers exhibits in this novel many of the properties of the ballad. Its plot is direct and swift; the action is familiar, rooted in folk tradition; and the language, stylized and intense, derives a quality of artifice from McCullers' studied use of archaic words and phrases. The narrator presents himself as a balladeer with much starkness of vision, an individual who establishes a desolate beginning and end for his tale, before he expands upon the intervening action, which he summarizes quickly in his opening words:

> The owner of the place was Miss Amelia Evans. But the person most responsible for the success and gaiety of the place was a hunchback called Cousin Lymon. One other person had a part in the story of this cafe—he was the former husband of Miss Amelia, a terrible character who returned to the town after a long term in the penitentiary, caused ruin, and then went on his way again. The cafe has long since been closed, but it is still remembered. (4)

Although he is responsible for the lively atmosphere in the cafe and provides his townsmen with food, drink, and fellowship, Lymon accentuates the sinister, as well as the comic, tone of the novel. One evening at dusk this dwarf hunchback trudges into the town and identifies himself as Miss Amelia's cousin. The villagers sitting on Miss Amelia's steps find him repulsive: "His hands were like dirty sparrow claws" (7). (McCullers, in fact, uses bird imagery throughout the novel to describe Lymon.) Because Miss Amelia thought that she had no relatives—a situation which sets her apart from other people—she is filled with wonder by the dwarf's insistent claim of kinship. She offers him a drink from the bottle in her overalls pocket "to liven his gizzard" (she owns the best still in the whole region), and she receives the weeping little man into her house.

Miss Amelia is a sorceress of reputation and establishes by her acts and attributes the ineffable atmosphere and eerie tone of the novel. She heals the diseases of the townfolk with her magical potions, and she regulates important events in their lives by telling them, for example, when the weather or the moon will be right for planting crops or for slaughtering hogs. Whenever her hated ex-husband, Marvin Macy, or her beloved dwarfed companion, Cousin Lymon, challenges her power and omniscience, the townspeople grow fearful and surly. While they respect her, they reveal curiosity and excitement about her, rather than deep concern. In their lack of affection, they become a vaguely malevolent force and, as it were, a sinister chorus to comment on the action. Consequently, when the townspeople do not see Lymon for the next three days, they assume that Amelia has murdered him. A self-appointed contingent arrives to investigate, and at this dramatic moment, Lymon makes a grand entrance from the top of the staircase, dressed in Amelia's fancy green shawl, which trails to the floor. He carries what the townsmen, astonished, recognize as the snuff box Amelia treasures because it belonged to her father. Lymon has filled it with cocoa and sugar, which he uses throughout the novel to sweeten his mouthful of decayed teeth.

McCullers' juxtaposition of past and present is notable. The narrator, soon after the opening sequence, moves back in time to reveal Amelia as she was at twenty, ten years before, when her father was still alive and cherished her. He had protected her, talked philosophically to her, and ridiculously nicknamed her "Little"; she slept calmly every night, as if covered with "warm axle grease." The narrator then dwells upon Amelia's present wealth, her ability to brew a liquor with magical properties, and her knowledge of folk medicine. Handsome enough to attract men, she is dark, tall, and muscular. She is a personage to be respected, not to be loved or pitied. Her chief recreation—bringing a lawsuit whenever she has a gambler's hunch that she may win it—suggests her selfishness and her shrewd eye for business.

A solitary individual, Amelia lacks any genuine basis for communication with either men or women. She has never cared for men, nor does she in this tale ever have a conversation with a woman; in fact, this book contains little direct conversation, the narrator more often summarizing the action. Amelia will not treat "female complaints," and blushes whenever talk of them arises. She also wears men's overalls. Though she denies her own femininity, she expresses maternal concern for children and is infinitely gentle in her treatment of them, making sure they are thoroughly anesthetized by drinking enough of her best liquor before she performs any painful operation.

Amelia's unconsummated marriage to Marvin Macy suggests that her denial of feminine identity may prevent her response to physical love from any man. In a large family of unwanted and abused children, Marvin Macy grew up with a stone in place of a heart, and as a young man he violated virgins throughout the land. Inexplicably, he falls in love with Amelia, reforms, and becomes suddenly humble. To the further astonishment of the townspeople, Amelia, soon after the death of her father, agrees to marry Macy. Awkward and uncomfortable in her wedding dress, Amelia amuses the guests as she reaches for the pockets of her overalls to rest her hands in them. In the days after the wedding, the mood of the villagers shifts dramatically from surprise and amusement to shock when they recognize that Amelia denies Macy access to her bedroom, abuses her lovesick groom, and finally orders him off her property.

If Amelia gains some sympathy at the beginning and the end of the book, at the point of her marriage she is almost monstrous, the female who preys upon the male whom she has lured to her abode. Though the townspeople react with disbelief to her humiliation of Macy, they also derive perverse pleasure from the fact that "someone has been thoroughly done in by some scandalous and terrible means" (31). They are tainted by the evil that Amelia herself seems to have let loose in the community.

Vengeance pervades the latter part of the tale when Macy returns to inflict vengeance upon the woman who has betrayed his love. In building toward the physical struggle between Amelia and Macy, which provides the climax for the book, the narrator slows the pace. About six years altogether pass between Lymon's appearance in town and his departure. Lymon immediately falls in love with Amelia's ex-husband and, because Macy does not accept this love, Lymon sits mourning on the porch rail, "like a bird on a telephone wire." Amelia must bury her pride and give Macy the best room in her house, to prevent Lymon's leaving with him. She concludes: "It is better to take in your mortal enemy than face the terror of living alone" (56).

Tension builds from August to Ground Hog Day, when the great confrontation takes place between Macy and Amelia, a struggle with overtones of the Grendel-Beowulf encounter. The townspeople are "recklessly glad" as they anticipate the battle between Amelia and Macy, a struggle of interminable length because of the mythical strength possessed by each antagonist. Only the intercession of the demonic Lymon, a still more powerfully mythical figure, finally defeats Amelia in the agonizingly protracted wrestling contest. A creature who vaguely possesses the characteristics of a pet, as well as human (or subhuman) attributes, Lymon now, like a hawk propelling himself through the air, leaps on Amelia's back, digs his birdlike claws into her shoulders, and helps to overcome her. Victorious after battle, Macy and Lymon steal Amelia's treasures and pillage her home and her still. Amelia waits three lonely years for Lymon to return at dusk before she boards up forever the windows of her dilapidated building. As at the beginning of the novel, the men of the prison chain gang can be heard singing as they work on the highway—twelve people who have escaped the solitary existence—but who are together only because they are in chains.

Spontaneous and lasting fellowship is an impossibility in this novel. The forced and uneasy fellowship in the cafe, like the harmony and solidarity of the chain gang, lacks genuineness.

The novel is remarkable for its sweep over wide reaches of time while it also achieves much compression and concentration. Four years elapse between Part I, when Lymon arrives, and Part II when he and Amelia are seen operating the cafe and talking in the long evenings together. Two years elapse between Part II and Part III, when trouble settles in upon Amelia as Lymon falls in love with her enemy.

II   Gothic, Mythical, and Ballad Aspects of the Novel

McCullers claimed that in *The Ballad of the Sad Cafe* she tried to illustrate the superiority of Agapé (communal affection) over Eros (passionate love). Actually, the novel demonstrates the destructive nature of Eros in the lives of the three main characters, Miss Amelia Evans, Cousin Lymon, and Marvin Macy. McCullers' suggestion of Agapé is at best minimal, and appears only in the brief and uncertain pleasure the villagers enjoy at the cafe. Even more elusive than the fickle Eros, Agapé provides a joy to be savored in passing, rather than a durable influence through which one might shape a lifetime. The townspeople develop no continuing sense of community but remain easily frightened and suspicious of Amelia and Cousin Lymon. They rise to no significant realization of Agapé, even if the tenuous fellowship they find at the cafe provides a few moments of satisfaction in the meaningless repetition of their days. But perhaps Agapé does win out by implication, for it is surely superior to the destructiveness of Eros as it is dramatized in this book.

In demonstrating the destructive nature of Eros in the lives of Amelia, Macy, and Lymon, McCullers implies that any three-sided love affair, particularly a bisexual one, can be expected to fail, and, beyond this, most love affairs between two people will not endure.

McCullers' theme of the isolated individual seeking escape from loneliness through love, which had inspired *The Heart Is a Lonely Hunter*, became exceedingly complex by the time she wrote this third novel. In her first novel, she had presented loneliness as an affliction of the solitary "hunter," who may possibly be cured by love and certainly can be cured by nothing else. But she indicated even in that novel, through the other characters' attraction to Singer, that love is often mere narcissism and that any individual craves response from an admiring lover primarily to reinforce his or her self-esteem. Such characters want not so much to love as to be loved. Only Antonapoulos eludes Singer's love, and ironically only he is beloved by Singer. In McCullers' second novel, *Reflections in a Golden Eye*, lust rather than love dominates the vortex of sadism, masochism, self-pity, and violence so dramatically presented. In *The Ballad of the Sad Cafe* she again addressed the dominant theme of her first novel: the ambiguity in love. The beloved resents and fears the lover, though he also needs him and craves his presence. Love, because it reveals one's inmost identity, causes the lover and the beloved to be psychologically vulnerable to each other and even more accessible to betrayal by any third person who may gain access to their private world. In a forthright passage, the narrator acknowledges the inescapable power of such paradoxical attraction and repulsion: "There are the lover and the beloved, but these two come from different countries. . . . The beloved fears and hates the lover, and with the best of reasons. For the lover is forever trying to strip bare his beloved" (24 - 25).

Thus love becomes in this novel a force which drives the lover into deeper isolation by driving him in on himself. Love is the dreadful result of an individual's isolation and its intensifier, rather than its cure. Eros, if frustrated, leads to hatred and destruction; Agapé is an ideal, an inspiriting influence seldom to be attained as a pure and lasting force, though it alone can give order and meaning to our chaotic lives.

Because it embodies qualities of the gothic as McCullers defined them in "The Russian Realists and Southern Literature," *The Ballad of the Sad Cafe*, like *Reflections in a Golden Eye*, is interesting to consider as evidence that she herself turned rapidly toward the gothic mode after she wrote this essay. The kind of novel written in this mode, she continued, is antithetical to the meticulous and reportorial depiction of character and milieu which she found, perhaps mistakenly, typical of most contemporary Southern fiction. In her view, it was imprecise and simplistic to apply the term "gothic" to such complex works as William Faulkner's *As I Lay Dying* largely on the basis of their combination of beauty and the sinister and their juxtaposition of the comic and the tragic, although Faulkner's works contain elements of the gothic as she defined them and as she began to use them in her own work.

In her presentation of situation and characters in *The Ballad of the Sad Cafe*, McCullers herself dramatically blends realistic detail with romantic and supernatural elements. Like gothic novelists, as she defined them, she herself attains striking effects of ambivalence in her work through presenting Amelia's tragic betrayal by Lymon within a comic frame and through the use of everyday phrases, perhaps more typical of the comic mode, to convey the despair reflected in the latter part of the book.

Gothic fiction writers in England at the close of the eighteenth century maintained that fear distorts the perceptions of the psyche and that a phenomenon ordinarily discerned by the rational mind as trivial can become, under stress, momentarily overpowering both for the character and the reader. These early gothic authors often deliberately chose medieval settings, because they could thus embed their credulous characters in an age and milieu wherein unquestioning belief in miracles, visions, necromancy, and dreams was common. Such a world predisposes the characters to be sensitive to extrasensory perceptions and to see the normal as through a distorting lens. Frequently, these individuals confuse the probable with the improbable.

In *Reflections in a Golden Eye* McCullers localized the action by limiting it to a military base, in order to suggest the presence of a closed society. The characters are further enclosed by their lack of emotional and intellectual development. They are limited by their intense obsessions or "simple-mindedness." Their personal limitations and their narrowed environment predispose them to irrational fear when they are under pressure. Thus, even in writing *Reflections in a Golden Eye*, McCullers showed her understanding that fundamental to the gothic mode of fiction is the creation of psychic stress in the characters that will distort their perceptions and also will, in turn, communicate intimations of a psychic realm that transcends the ordinary.

By the time she produced *The Ballad of the Sad Cafe*, she thoroughly understood the "gothic" principle that irrational impulses of all sorts distort an individual's perception of reality. The result is that in extreme circumstances the character will find a trivial or harmless phenomenon overpowering. In both *Reflections in a Golden Eye* and *The Ballad of the Sad Cafe*, McCullers renders states of inner turmoil in terms of outward stress or in terms of the terrifying, the macabre, or the bizarre. Another aspect of traditional gothic fiction that now appealed to McCullers was the dramatization of forces of evil at large in the universe, beyond the control and understanding of the characters. Evil in both McCullers' second and third books appears as an unmotivated, irrational, or inexplicable phenomenon. She appreciated, furthermore, the power of such forces and probed their psychological effects on the individual more fully than did earlier romantic novelists exploring this mode. Her characters react irrationally in their frustrations or their anxiety and seem as fascinated by evil as repelled by it. She also assumes, as did many early gothic writers, that a close relationship exists between evil and human solitude or loneliness.

Although in McCullers' first novel Singer cannot survive his anguish, she emphasized the optimism of Mick Kelly and Portia Copeland in the face of suffering. In *Reflections in a Golden Eye* and in *The Ballad of the Sad Cafe* she recognized more decisively that irrationality and evil lie as close to the heart of human experience as do the hunger for love and its possible redemptive influence. Whoever acknowledges that the cosmos is malign (or even sees that it is indifferent to the individual human being) may learn to laugh at it, she felt, may also learn to accept the fact that life is strange, uncomfortable, and never fully meaningful in human and rational terms, and may further realize that effort and inertia are equally powerless to change the universe.

In *The Ballad of the Sad Cafe*, as in her first novel, the principal character remains a lonely hunter after a brief period of love expended upon an unlovable and unresponsive person. Pity for others and the desire to achieve a meaningful communion with them is absent, moreover, as the isolation in the lives of Amelia, Macy, and Lymon intensifies. In *The Ballad of the Sad Cafe* isolation, fear, and guilt also return to the lives of the townspeople after the struggle between Amelia and Macy leaves her defeated.

Even though McCullers in *The Ballad of the Sad Cafe* projects her characters more decidedly into a fantastic milieu than she did in *Reflections in a Golden Eye*, paradoxically the figures in *The Ballad of the Sad Cafe* emerge as more individualized figures and as people more often worthy of sympathy than those presented in the earlier book. In addition to being grotesques or eccentrics, Amelia, Lymon, and Macy sometimes reach universal and archetypal dimensions, as they reflect certain complexities in human relationships and the strong individual's insight into his or her own situation.

All the characters illustrate these challenging complexities. The giantlike Amelia, foolishly but lovingly nicknamed "Little" by her father, is, as an adult, afraid to assume her full sexual identity and

remains his little child. Lymon, the hunchbacked dwarf, openly
weeps for himself, longs for a male lover, and finds pleasure in in-
citing trouble among other individuals, but he also has a shrewd
sense of the realities that encompass him. Of all the characters,
Lymon's behavior is the least predictable; his motivation, the most
paradoxical and ironic. He is both more and less than a man, neither
adult nor child, neither sparrow and hawk nor quite human. Injured
irreparably as a small child by poverty and by his parents' mistreat-
ment, Macy, in his turn, regresses to rebellion, self-destruction, and
vengefulness when he encounters rejection in his marriage; but he
also elicits sympathy as a victim of forces which are too powerful for
him to control. His behavior, likewise, is at times far from the ordinary, since he exists with only a stone where his heart had been;
he cannot react in the usual human mode when his emotions are involved.

Amelia is also an unusual and complicated individual. In spite of
the comic means used by McCullers to characterize her, she
becomes a figure capable of deep and poignant suffering. She is the
one who symbolizes most forcibly the inevitable isolation experienced by most persons—an isolation which may be the result of
their self-centered behavior. She has been set apart at the beginning
by the townspeople as a woman with special understandings and
powers, and at the end she is isolated as one who, through a series of
peculiar incidents and relationships, has been overcome by incomprehensible forces of evil.

Like the anonymous townspeople, the three chief characters, in
spite of their legendary powers, are intense, irrational, superstitious,
and naive. Amelia hides her uncertainty behind her shrewd business
activity and her ability to take risks in her law suits, but even she is
fearful of what she perceives as supernatural messages manifested
in natural events or objects. The townspeople are childlike, simplistic, easily frightened by events or objects which they do not
understand but also easily delighted by small pleasures, like the
bright decorations in the cafe. Such lack of sophistication makes
McCullers' presentation of them as superstitious and suspicious all
the more credible. They are bound by long traditions of folk-
knowledge, some of which are terrifying, some of which are amusing, and some of which provide colorful language and imagery for
McCullers' tale.

The cafe becomes a joyous place where poor people, trapped in monotonous work in the textile mill, can see themselves as individuals of some worth; but this sense of worth grows in them only through the potency of Miss Amelia's liquor, which provides warmth and which also has the magical power to heal, to kill pain, and even to produce sexual potency. Amelia herself does not seem to know the exact significance of the acorn that she picked up the afternoon her father died when Cousin Lymon questions her about it, but the narrator hints that perhaps it symbolizes masculinity, her father's love, or his death. Likewise, the significance of the kidney stone removed from Amelia's body assumes special awesomeness for her, perhaps because it caused her the greatest pain she experienced before the agony of Lymon's desertion. Throughout the book, the villagers perceive various phenomena as mysterious portents. For example, the snowfall which bewilders Amelia, as well as the townsfolk, freezes her spirit into silence so that her speech sounds muffled—her aborted speech reflects her benumbed inner being. The snowfall is surely an omen, but one she cannot interpret to her satisfaction.

Most dramatic in its resemblance to folk legends which glorify the heroic is the climactic fight between Amelia and Macy, which achieves dimensions far beyond the natural and the ordinary. Bird imagery presages this struggle: "A hawk with a bloody breast flew over the town and circled twice around the property of Miss Amelia" (28). The conquest occurs on Ground Hog Day, a day of portent. Lymon early that morning takes a solitary journey into the swampland to see whether the animal sees his shadow, much as a character in mythology might sojourn into the netherworld to gain knowledge about his own fate and destiny. Because the weather is "neither rainy nor sunny but with a neutral temperature" (58), the groundhog casts an indeterminate image and so foreshadows the long impasse of the wrestling match. The deliberate, ceremonial decorum of the antagonists lends solemnity to the event: "They walked toward each other with no haste, their fists already gripped, and their eyes like the eyes of dreamers" (60 - 61). At one point, the narrator turns from the deadlocked belligerents to describe imperturbably the other spectators. When he finally returns to the match, he soberly exaggerates the length of time in which the struggle has hung in balance: "Perhaps it was half an hour before the course of the fight shifted. Hundreds of blows had been exchanged, and there was still a deadlock" (62). Little dramatic action occurs in the book except for this great event of extraordinary violence. Anticipation, memory, and long anxiety are far more important in creating intensity and ominousness than the incidents themselves.

As later in *The Member of the Wedding*, the frequent, unexplained, and incantatory repetition of the numbers *three* and *seven* suggests magical or religious ritual. The numbers appear in many connections. For three days and three nights after Lymon's arrival, the townspeople do not see him. Repeatedly, the narrator claims three good persons live in town, but their identity remains secret, as does that of the three persons who are said to come from Society City to see the fight. After her dramatic fight, Amelia knocks her fist on her desk three times and then begins to sob. Three years she waits for Lymon to return before boarding up her house. Her medicines may be efficacious because the number *seven* appears in the directions: seven swallows of water for hiccups, seven runs around the millpond for crick in the neck, and seven doses of Amelia's Miracle Mover for curing worms. Macy's cruelty derives from his upbringing as one of seven unwanted children. Seven times Amelia invites Lymon to go with her to Cheehaw, on the fateful day that he stays home alone, meets Macy, and falls in love with him. The townfolk know intuitively that the climactic and brutal struggle which forces Amelia to acknowledge Macy's mastery will take place at 7:00 that evening.

The attribution of magical properties to certain numbers occurs in folklore of many cultures. This ritualistic use of numbers suggests a universal significance to this tale that extends it far beyond the life of one woman in an obscure village. The narrator's archaic formality also hints at a wider significance in the story he tells.

The novel contains relatively little dialogue. Hence, the narrator's voice becomes particularly important in establishing shifts in tone or mood.[3] His acknowledgment of the efficacy of incantatory rhythms in the repetition of certain numbers reflects his willingness to share the superstitions of the naive villagers. He thus gives credence to the villagers' beliefs, and he himself seems to believe in the gossip that they pass about, exaggerated and malicious as it may be. The narrator shifts unpredictably from using the voice of a laborer at the mill, talking after work with an audience of other bored mill hands, to using the voice of a mystical balladeer who speaks in a poetic, archaic, and stylized pattern. The balladeer's omniscience and his primitive sensibility seem inconsistent with the colloquial voice of the millworker, though they both ultimately reveal a folk origin. As poetic singer, he remarks, for instance, that Macy upon his return from prison "caused ruin" (4). But the colloquial idiom, comic in its emphasis, dominates most of the narrative passages. The humor in them gains much of its ludicrous effect from a colorful vocabulary, a curious phrasing, or a use of surprising illustrations. In his simple and direct sentences, the narrator, on the other hand, often eloquently expresses his philosophy as oracular wisdom. He moves in a moment from the comic to the profound.

The contrast between the comic idiom and the poetic expression in the narrative voice may be illustrated in the descriptions of Amelia's wonderful brew. When her liquor is not available, the narrator complains sadly that all other whiskey in the region is of such poor quality that "those who drink it grow warts on their liver the size of goobers" (63). In contrast to such colloquial comic imagery, the narrator elsewhere describes Amelia's liquor in highly poetic context. For instance, it can make the spinner or weaver, whose sensitivity is long dulled by monotonous work, take a marsh lily in the palm of his hand and discover in it a significance that warms his soul. As an invisible message written in lemon juice becomes visible when held under the warmth of a lamp, so the mysteries of the universe, the narrator asserts, can be seen through the magical warmth of Amelia's brew. Her liquor opens astonishing worlds to the townspeople. Beyond "the loom, the dinner pail, the bed and then the loom again," a man can "see for the first time the cold, weird radiance of a midnight January sky, and a deep fright at his own smallness stops his heart" (9 - 10).

In addition to the narrator's continual shifting between the colloquial and the formal or poetic, his style is characterized throughout the book by an extensive use of lists, as if his credibility could best be increased by piling up factual details. After the climactic fight, for example, the narrator takes time to itemize the damage done to Amelia's property by Lymon and Macy. Whenever a meal is eaten, the narrator lists the menu, which includes the regional favorites: "fried chicken . . . mashed rootabeggars, collard greens, and hot pale golden sweet potatoes" (10). He lists the names of all the eight men who call on Amelia early in the story to investigate the rumor that she has murdered Lymon, although we hear of none of them elsewhere in the tale. (Some of the details in these lists may be humorously irrelevant to the rest of the items in the series, a comic device used by McCullers in *Reflections in a Golden Eye*.)

The explicitness by which the narrator establishes Amelia's milieu helps him gain credence for Amelia as an inhabitor of that milieu and as an extraordinary personage. Though the exact sources of her remarkable power remain mysterious, that power is so carefully demonstrated and her fabulous reputation is so convincingly documented that one cannot question the validity of her legendary accomplishments. The narrator always presents her behavior, her feelings, her thoughts, her appearance, and her words concretely rather than in the abstract. For instance, instead of remarking that Amelia was energetic and extremely busy in the autumn before Macy's return, the narrator recites a long series of her activities, comic in its specificity and variety:

She made a new and bigger condenser for her still, and in one week ran off enough liquor to souse the whole country. Her old mule was dizzy from grinding so much sorghum, and she scalded her Mason jars and put away pear preserves. . . . She had traded for three tremendous hogs, and intended to make much barbecue, chitterlins, and sausage. . . . One day she sat down to her typewriter and wrote a story—a story in which there were foreigners, trap doors, and millions of dollars. (42)

Such a passage, with its celebration of a woman possessing remarkable vitality and zest, renders more poignant the effect of both the first and the last pages of this work, wherein the languor of life in the late summer afternoon town dominates. The narrator closes the tale, as he began it, by commenting quietly upon the twelve men on the chain gang, who represent, in part, the dull existence and the tragic boredom that ordinarily prevail in this town. As they sing, they leave behind them, for the moment, their misery. They begin to work in the early dawn. The ordinary daily routine of hard work and a suggestion of the eerie in their music—sounds which seem to emanate from both earth and air—contrast strangely, as do the black sky and the streaks of the golden sunrise and the skin of the black men and white. Disaster in their lives and peacefulness in their monotonous activity find expression in this "music intricately blended, both somber and joyful" (66).

Even more a prisoner now than these men, Amelia exists as an idle and remote presence behind the shutters of the dilapidated house on the now deserted street. At the close, she thus becomes more abstract, a mythic figure representing the deep, chronic isolation which McCullers saw at the center of human life. Her face, dimly peering out from the darkness, is "sexless" because loneliness surrounds men and women alike. Because the most isolated people may become almost invisible, her face is like "the terrible dim faces" one sees only in dreams.

CHAPTER 5

The Member of the Wedding *(1946)*

I *The Search for Poetic Precision and Harmony*

DURING the five years McCullers struggled with her short novel *The Member of the Wedding,* she lived through tumultuous and insistent distractions. She left this book for several months to write *The Ballad of the Sad Cafe.* She faced exigencies of illness, bereavement, and divorce; and the war provided intense anxieties. In the process of creating her twelve-year-old protagonist, Frankie Addams, McCullers suffered from the vivid recollection of her own adolescence. What she had half-consciously perceived as abandonment by a surrogate parent when her music teacher left Georgia, she now relived as she projected her anger and grief into Frankie when she is abandoned by the bride and groom.

McCullers' lifelong sense of herself as different from other people, and consequently as peculiarly isolated, pervades all of her books. Here the portrayal of Frankie's distress grows even more poignant than does that of young Mick Kelly in *The Heart Is a Lonely Hunter,* perhaps because the autobiographical element became for McCullers more insistent. Unlike Mick Kelly, Frances in "Wunderkind," and the adolescent Carson McCullers herself, Frankie Addams does not aspire to the concert stage. But McCullers envisioned Frankie as a person extraordinarily sensitive to sound and silence and as one who continually relates music to her mood, her developing philosophy, and her situation.

Even if McCullers' personal life had been less turbulent between 1941 and 1946 and even if the pain of remembering her own growing up had been less sharp, the complex literary challenges posed by this compressed and deceptively simple work might explain the length of time she required for its creation, in contrast to the
80

rapidity with which she composed her three earlier books. McCullers saw this novel and the play which developed from it as "poetic" compositions comprised of "fugue-like" passages. In the elusive changes of mood, the relationships among characters, the interplay among themes, and the interweaving of theme and metaphor, she sought, she said, "precision and harmony" much as a poet would.[1]

The novel and the play depend for their impact upon the characterization of Frankie and Berenice Sadie Brown, a middle-aged black who keeps house for Frankie's father, as they encounter conflict and bewildering change both within themselves and in the world surrounding them. The dramatic action is complex, because each of the two figures is treated as a composite of the many unreconciled identities within her individual psyche. Consequently, Frankie, anxiously entering adolescence, must emerge in every scene as simultaneously child and adult. Berenice, whether joyous or in agony, must emerge as imperious and vital, although she is, like Frankie, several selves struggling in a fragmented spirit. A woman of imposing significance in the eyes of Frankie and her six-year-old cousin, John Henry West, Berenice becomes for them at different times the affectionate or stern mother, the primitive seer, and the black queen who once lived with her dream-lover, Ludie Freeman, in a beautiful land of ice and snow. In her perception of herself, Berenice possesses an even broader range of identities: the grieving widow, the insulted divorcee, the battered and disfigured wife, the woman fearful of aging, the exploited black servant, the woman who greatly enjoys sex, and the perennially hopeful bride. Fearful of aging, Berenice loves still to play with children, and she sees herself most clearly as a young bride. She has chosen an artificial blue eye (after a beating by her fourth husband mutilated her own eye), and she perhaps attempts to achieve in this choice a linking of the worlds of the Negro and the white. In the utopian vision which she articulates whenever she and the children take turns being "Holy Lord God" and creating the world all over again, Berenice gives to all people dark skin and blue eyes.

Frankie can indulge the childlike part of her personality in playing with John Henry. As Mick Kelly in *The Heart Is a Lonely Hunter* could depend on her little brother, Bubber, Frankie can count on John Henry for support or for a willingness to listen to her anger and grief. Blinded by tears of anger because some girls have spread rumors that she smells bad, she feels his sticky little fingers caressing the back of her neck. If Frankie never becomes a full member of the wedding of her brother and his bride, John Henry never quite becomes a full member of the trio who spend every afternoon in Berenice's hot kitchen. He remains peripheral, often only an observer, a listener, or a questioner. But he refuses ever to be left out. He insists on playing the card games, but he will not follow the rules. He thinks it would be fun to be alternately a boy and a girl, and his behavior makes his age seem indeterminate. In his ambiguous identity as ageless and sexless, he functions in the plot somewhat as Anacleto does in *Reflections in a Golden Eye* or Lymon in *The Ballad of the Sad Cafe*. However, his development is much more rounded than theirs, and his emotional appeal as an engaging, if enigmatic, child relates him more clearly, perhaps, to Bubber in *The Heart Is a Lonely Hunter* or to the tag-along little boy in McCullers' early story "Sucker."

Amusing and spritelike, John Henry provides much comedy, but his death elicits from Berenice the grief, the sense of loss, and the shaken faith which dominate the ending. In contrast, Frankie's seeming lack of concern for her only playmate's death and her coldness to Berenice, as she ignores her farewell in order to chat superficially with a new friend, suggest a perhaps inevitable loss of sincerity and affectionate spontaneity as she moves from childhood to maturity. The characters have advanced from the complexity, grief, and conflict which they knew in the hot summer to the relative simplicity and stability promised by the autumn, but this apparently peaceful resolution is an uneasy one. The child, John Henry, is dead and the child who had lingered within Frankie is also gone.

The problems which distressed Frankie have been consequential. She has posed questions of metaphysical import and their significance has been validated, repeated, and enlarged in the struggles of the adult, Berenice. Through the intensity of McCullers' dramatizing of them, these issues have been projected beyond the trio to all human beings. The stress within Frankie and Berenice and the basic antagonism in their explosive encounters with each other reflect, at least tangentially, the violence of a world at war. Frankie's willingness, finally, to ignore all unanswered questions at the close of the book suggests that she has, in fact, failed to develop in any genuine sense. A superficial self-assurance, along with heightened insensitivity and complacency, pass for maturity.

The slowly cumulative characterization of the kitchen trio and the intricate mounting and balancing of several themes, all of which are projected into a rich and unifying imagery, make this book abundantly complex in its philosophical and emotional range.[2] Nevertheless, *The Member of the Wedding* has a remarkably simple structure. Both climactic events—the wedding of Jarvis and Janice and the death of John Henry—occur with startling abruptness. Nearly all the action and dialogue take place during one weekend in August and in Berenice Sadie Brown's kitchen. Only Frankie, John Henry, and Berenice command attention. Frankie's father seldom appears; her mother is dead. Frankie's point of view and voice dominate, although John Henry's affectionate teasing and Berenice's admonitions and scoffing at the girl's dramatic declarations provide balance and perspective.

The three have spent every afternoon of the summer playing cards and talking. Ominously in the summer silence, they wait but do not know for what they wait. Behind the walls, decorated with crayon drawings of plane wrecks and other catastrophes scrawled large, the rats scratch endlessly. At times, the three sit tensely listening to the water drip in the sink, hearing the slap of the cards on the table, or even becoming frightened by the sound of their own breathing.

Their anxious waiting mirrors the nation's anxieties during that summer as it waits for the shift in the balance of power in the war, while few suspect that mankind is about to split the atom, with all the possibilities for destruction that that event will bring about. The kitchen radio is never turned off, in case some news may filter through what Frankie calls "sweet sleazy music." Jarvis, Frankie's brother, and the soldier who takes her to the Blue Moon bar are both on army leave. Frankie opens the newspaper and cries out that Americans are in Paris. One of the "seven dead people she knew," whom she systematically lists to impress herself and the others with the awesomeness of her experience, is a young neighbor killed recently in battle.[3]

One weekend late in August after the long waiting with time seeming to stand still, Frankie can shout, "Oh, Jesus. . . . The world is certainy a sudden place!" (614)[4] Jarvis arrives from Alaska with news that he will marry Janice in nearby Winter Hill on Sunday. Frankie immediately adopts a new name—*F. Jasmine*—because women who are part of a wedding change their names as they enter a "joined" life. After the Sunday celebration, she will be united in a *Ja* trinity—Jasmine, Jarvis, and Janice; and the lonely Frankie will no longer exist. The old kitchen trio will be dissolved.

In its place, the wedding will publicly acknowledge her new identity, exactly as a christening publicly acknowledges the naming of a newly born personality. On Saturday F. Jasmine buys a fancy orange satin dress for the ceremony, and discovers a state of security and elation she has never known—her "wedding frame of mind" in which she understands the "joined" life or the "we of me" she has waited for throughout her "scared spring" and "crazy summer." She finds herself suddenly able to talk confidently to strangers about the wedding plans and to look them in the eye. Previously only when she had looked into the eyes of freaks in the carnival or passed the barred windows of the jail and her eyes met those of prisoners had she felt recognized as a kindred being. As a *Ja* she is no longer a freak or prisoner, and her new gregariousness attracts the interest of a young soldier, who takes her to a bar and invites her to his cheap hotel room. Because his sexual advances, which she has unwittingly encouraged, frighten her, she cracks a water pitcher over his head and runs away. The experiences of this night make her in every way see that she has crossed the line and left childhood behind. But she is also disturbed because she cannot maintain her sense of the *Ja* life. She discovers that she still wants to confide in John Henry but no longer can. If she is now a murderer who will be forever pursued by "the law," she cannot share her crime with a child. John Henry may utter the terrible oath she at first demands: "If I tell, I hope God will sew up my mouth and sew down my eyes and cut off my ears with the scissors" (763). But he still could not be depended upon, because he would not understand. She might as well argue with cement as try to impress Berenice and John Henry, Frankie thinks.

On Sunday the wedding is suddenly over—in two sentences McCullers relates that the event was "wrecked. . .unmanaged as a nightmare. By midafternoon it was all finished and the return bus left at four o'clock. . . . Frances wanted the whole world to die" (768). She is disillusioned,, because she has not achieved the *Ja* identity she has striven for during her F. Jasmine phase. Though she now assumes her legal name, *Frances,* she is again the scared, crazy, and unjoined Frankie, and she angrily mourns her loss on the way home. Ironically, in her desolation she turns her back on those with whom she has actually been "joined" and refuses the comfort that Berenice, John Henry, or her father could have offered her. That night she runs away but lingers around the dark streets, as if postponing the leaving behind of both town and childhood. At the

Blue Moon bar, her father and "the law" easily capture her, since she has all along apparently been unwilling to leave the physical and spiritual terrain familiar to her.

The book closes precipitously. It is October. Frankie has entered a new school, and she has a friend with whom she can gossip. Just as the wedding took place parenthetically, so now the death of John Henry occurs between chapters, and the reader learns that the child has died of meningitis after a few days of terrible pain. Grieving for John Henry and for her jailed half-brother, Honey, Berenice now prepares for a settled life with a fifth husband, "a good, colored gentleman" who cannot make her "shiver." She no longer will demand a husband like her first one, Ludie. Some of Berenice's dreams have died, as have Frankie's, and death itself has triumphed over John Henry. A mundane, and somewhat complacent and insensitive, maturity begins to dominate Frankie, whose imagination, humor, wild hopes, and fears had enlivened her "scared spring" and "crazy summer."

II *"Go and Behold Yourself": Berenice as Frankie's Mirror*

If this novella presented only the conflicts within the life of Frankie and their partial resolution as she matures through a crisis, McCullers would undoubtedly have made use of more conventional methods to portray the "rites of passage" from childhood to adult society. She would still have achieved a work of significant insight into the psyche of the female early adolescent. The unusual achievement of this book, however, resides in McCullers' depiction of Frankie, though in many ways a typical adolescent, as a freak and a prisoner. The aesthetic distinction of the book derives even more from McCullers' skilled refraction of Frankie's conflicts against those of Berenice Sadie Brown.[5] The "precision and balance" which McCullers continually sought in writing this novella lie most notably in her skilled revelation of Berenice and Frankie through their almost continuous contact with each other. (In the play this effect is even more concentrated, because all of the scenes take place in the kitchen or adjoining yard. The Blue Moon scenes and the wedding—which occurs in the Addams's living room—are reported to Berenice as events which take place offstage.) The problems and responses of Frankie, echoed in those of the older Berenice, achieve a universal significance, because they are seen to be the preoccupations and the aspirations of another generation and another race.

Though Frankie and Berenice experience similar fears and hopes, they often become extreme antagonists. Their differences are as great as their similarities. In the relationships existing between the two women, McCullers can dramatize most effectively the conflicts between black and white, between old and young, and even between mother and daughter. Berenice's hostility is barely smothered in her patronizing remarks to Frankie: "I believe the sun has fried your brains" (600), or "You jealous. . . . Go and behold yourself in the mirror. I can see from the color in your eye" (600). When Frankie, disgusted with her gangling appearance, cries, "I just wish I would die," Berenice, with no tenderness, replies, "Well, die then" (621). Frankie storms away from her and verbally, in turn, abuses John Henry. Repeatedly, Berenice mocks Frankie when she loses control and rages at herself and the whole world. Such condescension and harshness often succeed in getting Frankie back to reality and behaving sensibly: "I intend to sit by myself and think over everything for a while!" (620) she says, after one very stormy situation. At other times, Berenice's taunts arouse in Frankie more bitterness and violence than they curb. In one instance, Frankie's response is to throw a knife so fast across the kitchen that it embeds itself in a door, and in another scene, she threatens, "Some day you going to look down and find that big fat tongue of yours pulled out by the roots and laying there before you on the table" (637). Berenice's behavior toward Frankie is characterized as much by her shouting, "Devil!" at Frankie as by her inviting Frankie to climb into her lap when she feels most afraid and alone.

McCullers' "precision and balance" lie also in this skilled fusion of opposing emotions, like love and anger, which characterize the relationship throughout the book between Frankie and Berenice and, to a lesser degree, that between Frankie and her father and that between Frankie and John Henry. Ethel Waters may have brought Berenice in the stage play and motion picture too close to the "mammy" stereotype, for McCullers' conception of her is much more complex. Berenice energetically responds to the turmoil in Frankie; always strongly and sometimes negatively. Frankie, in turn, can fight more intensely the authority characterizing for her the adult world when it is represented in a servant than in a parent.

McCullers goes beyond a presentation of the antagonism between generations and beyond the two individuals to show the violent and complex conflicts both women experience within themselves. McCullers relates the war within Frankie's psyche to the inward war that Berenice experiences when she finally lets Ludie die, as she decides to marry a far different man, T.T. Williams, for his own goodness. When Frankie and Berenice talk philosophically and with deep emotion, one sometimes hears dynamic dialogue as the women clash with each other and alternately reveal the anger and the tenderness they feel for each other. More often, however, one hears a rising antiphony in which one woman speaks, the other speaks in a contrasting tone, and finally the two join to achieve unified utterance, sometimes revealing a deep accord, sometimes a frustrating inability to communicate. In these antiphonal scenes, the two women do not necessarily speak to each other or to John Henry. Rather each speaks aloud to herself or to a vaguely conceived and undefined audience, which may or may not include the other two people present.

A sophisticated curiosity and an acute speculativeness mark Frankie's thoughtful words, and it is partly her tragedy that she fails to sustain her originality of mind and lapses in the last pages into banal acceptance of convention. At times, she and Berenice share a surprising wisdom in their conversation; at other times, Berenice marvels at Frankie's foolishness. At times, she perceptively understands the child's mind. Frankie, who longs to be understood, paradoxically rages whenever the older woman understands her too well. Berenice can also deflect too easily, with her common sense and her jealousy of Frankie's youth, the girl's untamed aspirations.

When Berenice and Frankie talk about the mysteries of individuality and the vastness of the universe, they become so intent on sharing the other's insight that they feel in awe of each other when they recognize their closeness. Berenice is strongly moved, for example, when Frankie hesitantly divulges the momentary vision she had downtown that morning, the day before the wedding: Jarvis and Janice were in Winter Hill preparing for the wedding, but Frankie saw them, for a few seconds, walking beside her. Berenice is overwhelmed by Frankie's revelation, because she has herself at times had a glimpse of her dead first husband, Ludie, walking beside her. She had thought that she was the only human being in the world to have such a supernatural experience.

If one central theme of the book is Frankie's need to achieve a sense of identity with others, this sharing of a supernatural experience marks the closest approach to the imaginative conjoining of Frankie and Berenice. It is followed, in fact, by a kind of communion ceremony. Frankie reaches over and takes one of Berenice's

cigarettes. Berenice allows her to do so; for the first time, Frankie
sits smoking with an adult. Frankie and Berenice are at several
other times remarkably congruent in their preoccupations and insights, considering their antagonism and the fact that one lives in
anticipation while the other lives in memory. While Frankie waits
impatiently to move into adulthood, Berenice longs to return to the
past—the snowy winters in Cincinnati before her first husband,
Ludie, died. In the hot South, she has three times married men who
fleetingly reminded her of Ludie. (One wore Ludie's overcoat,
which she had sold to pay his funeral expenses; another merely had
a scarred thumb which looked like Ludie's.) Whenever Berenice
recounts for John Henry and Frankie the romantic saga that begins
with her meeting Ludie at sunset near a filling station and reaches
its height with her entertaining twenty-eight people at a fish fry,
sewing on a new machine, getting a fox fur for Christmas, and walking in snow in Cincinnati, the children see her transformed into a
queen, radiantly unrolling her life for them like a splendid bolt of
gold cloth.

III Fear of Independence: "The We of Me"

If the repulsion-attraction relationship between Frankie and
Berenice (and to a lesser extent between Frankie and John Henry,
provides one major strand in the novella, a second thematic concern
resides in Frankie's longing to become "joined"—to be a member
of a club, to have a close friend, to donate her blood so that her life
will flow in the veins of people living all over the world. Even more
than her desire for adult independence, she wants ultimately to lose
individual identity through being assimilated into the *Ja* trinity at
the wedding ceremony. Early in the book her misery centers around
the conviction that she is set apart as a freak—the most "unjoined"
person in the universe, a person who is "a member of nothing in the
world." As this "separate" person, she regards herself as "dirty and
greedy and mean and sad" (682). Her thin body exposed in a BVD
undershirt and her hair chopped off like a little boy's, she clings to
careless childish ways, even though she is growing toward womanhood. She figures her growth rate for the last two months and
concludes that she will soon be nine feet tall; and she will then be
revealed for what she has long known herself to be—a freak.
Because she hates her body, she jabs with a kitchen knife at slivers
in her grubby bare feet and cries over her "rusty" elbows.

Anticipation of her identification with Jarvis and Janice gives her confidence—which she lacks as an individual—to reach out to strangers on Saturday morning. Though she tries to focus continually on a mental image of the three members of the wedding walking, inseparable and in harmony, beside a sunny glacial lake, she cannot, either in the bar or in the soldier's room, retain what she calls her "wedding frame of mind" (680), a state of feeling in which she draws close to her new "joined" state, "the we of me" (646). Her encounter with the soldier, rather than being a maturing experience, sends her back to her adolescent insecurity. Sexual naiveté, sexual guilt, and sexual interest all emerge in her behavior with the soldier, and her ignorance of sex is almost as great as John Henry's. Her sense of guilt is so confused by her ignorance of sex that the guilt is related to no specific and clearly understood act. The "law" may pursue her forever, because she has "just brained a crazy man" with a water pitcher after she has bitten his tongue, but her sense of guilt is for something greater and less explicit. She cannot explain her crime in confession to John Henry because he is a child, but she also cannot explain it to herself because she is still a child.

Because she cannot share the experience with John Henry, she escapes from reality that evening into her "wedding frame of mind." In her solitary meditation, she moves through snow, closely entwined with Janice and Jarvis and knows that, united in a mystical trinity, they will have "thousands and thousands and thousands of friends" and will belong to "more clubs than anyone can keep track of" (738).

Frankie's sexual ignorance and inexperience certainly might argue that the relationship she anticipates achieving with Jarvis and Janice after the wedding is mysterious, transcendent, and platonic, and quite remote from sexuality. In spite of Berenice's assumption that Frankie is jealous, her longing springs from no possessiveness about Jarvis or jealousy of Janice. Frankie's love for Jarvis, the warrior returned from the land of ice and snow, and her love for Janice, the beautiful stranger from Winter Hill, are equal in her mind. The union of the three will closely resemble her conception of what the dynamic marriage of Ludie Freeman and Berenice must have been: Ludie and Berenice lived for nine years a life of celebration because they were, as members of a wedding, truly joined. They understood what it is to attain "the we of me."

The elusive fantasies of her "wedding frame of mind" momentarily ease for Frankie the fear and distress of the past months. They replace her earlier fantasy of perfect membership attainable through the sharing of her blood as a Red Cross donor. She had then imagined her individuality lost "in the veins of Australians and fighting French and Chinese . . . as though she were close kin to all these people" (623). In that fantasy she saw herself decorated for contributing her life's blood to "join the war," while army officers sharply saluted and addressed her with respect as "Addams," because her act of courage made her one of them.

Though Frankie longs for adventure and a degree of independence from her father, Berenice, and John Henry, she fears greatly her own individuality, because she perceives a solitary person to be one who has stepped, unprotected, into a universe which is indifferent and hostile to human pretensions. Being incontrovertibly joined with another person protects one, she thinks, provides him with direction, and allows him to move safely into the new and the unknown. One will, then, for a lifetime join clubs, go to parties, be interviewed for the newsreel as an "eye witness" and become part of a tightly organized society.

It is significant that Frankie refers as much to the cosmos as to the world; if the world is out of control and the war makes her see "bombed eyes and torn planes," she, like Berenice after John Henry's death, is uncertain about the power of God over the rest of the universe. She demands to be kept safely in orbit, not hurtling "loose" and alone as the world whirls faster. Just as she can no longer count on time moving predictably, she can no longer count on the stars staying in their course. Though freedom tempts her, she resists it, because she fears unrestricted individuality. Such freedom would, like John Henry's refusal to follow the rules of the card games, preclude control, design, and pattern. These she perceives as existing only where people are assimilated in orderly units—clubs, armies, or even marriages. While she tells Mary Littlejohn at the close of the book that she plans to be a great poet, she immediately qualifies it with her "safer" ambition—to be "the foremost radar expert in the world." Though bored with routine and highly imaginative, she wants less, at least at this point, to be a leader or an uncharted adventurer than to become one whose understanding of the laws of physics can keep planes and people from being "loose" in space.

Frankie's insistence on assured patterns, on repetition, or on circling around a fixed center dominate much of the book's imagery: metaphors such as radar, motors, musical rhythm, musical themes, card-game rules, and military regimentation. Frankie grows frantic if music lacks regular thematic pattern or stops short of a final measure or note on the scale. Her most reassuring possession is the old motor in her bedroom. When she is agitated, she turns it on and finds comfort in hearing its rhythmic hum and watching the gears move synchronically.

IV *"To Widen and Bust Free"*: *Berenice's Search for Freedom*

Though Berenice still longs for another marriage to match her perfect union with Ludie Freeman, she, unlike Frankie, is not willing to relinquish her freedom and individuality. She argues forcefully in favor of attaining independence—even of becoming a cashier in the restaurant owned by her prospective husband, where she will feel important in high-heeled shoes and tap her foot as she watches the customers. Because she recognizes that blacks have been more imprisoned by society than whites and because middle-aged people are more enmeshed in routine and dull responsibility than are the young, Berenice maintains that being caught is even worse than being loose. Blacks, she contends, are eager "to widen and bust free" (740). Nevertheless, Berenice, like Frankie, acknowledges the disadvantages of independence when she comments on the inevitable loneliness of the so-called free personality.

Berenice's wisdom, won from longer experience than Frankie's, has embraced the paradoxical reality that, if one can lose oneself in a good family or marital identification with another, one can fully discover and save oneself. She wistfully recalls, "When I was with Ludie, I didn't feel so caught" (741). Ludie Freeman's surname is surely symbolic. In the antithesis of Berenice's memory of a perfect wedding and Frankie's anticipation of one, the reader recognizes the vulnerability of those who choose to give up individuality in order to exist only as members of a family. The longing for freedom will remain alive in such a sacrifice of personal freedom, but the strength to reach for it may be impaired. Berenice gained a spiritual unity through her marriage to Ludie, but she achieved it at the cost of her self-sufficiency. At his death, part of herself was torn away and buried with him. Similarly, after the "wrecked" wedding at Winter Hill, Frankie continues to bear the pain of separate existence, but she can luckily look ahead to the attainment of the freedom and independence which a part of herself has continued to demand.

In the presentation of Berenice, the focus often shifts from the
psychological tragedy implicit in her widowhood to the configurations in American society—economic, racial, and family—which
further entrap her. We know that she is, as she says, "more caught"
because she is black in a society where whites have power. Honey,
her half-brother, may be often in jail because of some personal
deficiency; but he is also in trouble because racial intolerance, dis-
crimination, and poverty draw blacks toward crime. McCullers does
not focus intently in this book, as in her first and her last novels, on
economic and racial injustice, but concern for the poor or the black
provides a current which runs through the book, just as the war provides a consistently ominous background. When Berenice in her
half-crooning voice recites the story of her love with Ludie, a lurid
memory of another dead black male haunts Frankie's memory. A
boy, whose throat was slit, lay in the alley behind her father's store.
The open throat, people whispered, looked as if it were about to
speak or sing.

Berenice is caught because she is a black, a middle-aged person, a
woman, a widow, a divorcee, a victim of beatings, and a poor person. But Berenice is, in most of the book, a force of affirmation; and
she fights for happiness rather than resigning herself to the life of a
victim. She fights against being viewed as stereotypically old,
vigorously refusing to let Frankie call her an old woman. When
Frankie reminds her that she has been thirty-five for the last three
years, Berenice angrily retorts, "I still can ministrate" (698). She
may, at first, appear to be a sentimentalized maternal figure, but
she eagerly leaves her employer's house to meet her friends and "to
eat supper at the New Metropolitan Tea Room and sashay together
around the town" (628). She asserts, "I got as much right as
anybody to continue to have a good time so long as I can. . . . I
got many a long year ahead of me before I resign myself to a cor-
ner" (698). Even in her despair over John Henry and Honey at the
close of the book, she does not withdraw from making vigorous
decisions. If she cannot find another Ludie, she settles for the degree
of happiness she can find.

V   *The Mystery of Time: "Oh, Jesus, the World is*
Such a Sudden Place"

As Frankie and Berenice speculate in circular conversations about
such abstractions as freedom versus determinism, isolation versus a

desire for community, and living dangerously versus living cautiously, their views on individual identity reflect still another theme—a continuing confusion about the nature of time.

Time presents a particular mystery as it relates to the stages through which all individuals must pass. Frankie wonders how one can possibly remain the same person as a child and as an old person and how one can even be the same child in summer as in winter. Both Frankie and Berenice recognize the fascinating fact that any one person can be "reincarnated" as many different individuals at successive intervals throughout the course of a lifetime. For example, Frankie, F. Jasmine, and Frances are surely three separate, unreconciled identities as they move through one chaotic weekend. Also they are different from what they once were and from what they will be at some time in the future.

McCullers explores several themes related to the mystery of time—its varied pace, its relationship to the mutable and the immutable, its bearing upon the single and the manifold identities of each individual, and its role in bringing to fruition the human being at any point in his or her life. Whatever is unfinished or not yet defined frightens Berenice and Frankie and provides a recurring concern in their minds.

Whenever Berenice and Frankie sense that time itself stands suspended because an orderly process is interrupted before it is completed, they become excessively anxious. The card game halts in tenseness when the piano tuner stops one note short of completing the scale; Frankie beats her head with her fist when the jazz horn melody breaks off before a recurring theme; she cries, "I am sick unto death" when the card game cannot be finished after John Henry hides a card he thinks is pretty. Berenice mourns that Honey Camden Brown gets into trouble because the Creator withdrew His hand too soon when He made him. She also thinks that God left incomplete the sexual identity of Lily Mae Jenkins, a transvestite. Such metaphors of incompleteness recur throughout the novel, always arousing Berenice and Frankie. Most dramatic of the metaphors for the frustration of orderly development, progression, and life are the apparently senseless and untimely deaths of Ludie and John Henry.

In comic treatment of the theme, Berenice, Frankie, and John Henry pretend that they are the Trinity, and they recreate the world themselves in order to correct the errors that God has made in time. In doing so, they not only express their dissatisfaction but also reveal their individuality. Holy Lord God Berenice Sadie Brown announces the emergence of a new earth which is "just and round and reasonable," with no war, no murdered Jews, and Ludie Freeman always alive. Holy Lord God John Henry West excitedly describes his world in a high voice—one's arm can reach to California, everyone has an extra eye that can see a thousand miles, and dirt will be chocolate and rain, lemonade. Holy Lord God Frankie Addams creates a world wherein everyone has an airplane and a motorcycle, belongs to a world-inclusive club, can change sex at will, and may, upon request, go to a war island long enough to become a hero safely and without suffering.

Because time and imperfection remain a mystery, McCullers can affirm only time's mutability, indefiniteness, and inconclusiveness. Time stands still all summer, then in one weekend the world becomes for Frankie "a sudden place." No two days are the same length; in hot summer, time moves more slowly than in the invigorating winter. Time wonderfully moves backwards when Berenice tells of her good days with Ludie. It comfortingly stands still for a little while the night Frankie decides to run away but lingers around the dark streets of the town.

Even the structure of this book suggests the human perception of an erratic and unpredictable—rather than a controlled and unvarying—speed in the passage of time. For example, though the event has provided the entire focus of the book, the wedding is all over for the surprised reader in one sentence. Likewise, though John Henry has been one of the three main characters, the reader hears that his death occurred "offstage" between chapters.

To the end of the novel, McCullers continues with great "precision and harmony" to balance the turmoil and self-centered egotism of Frankie with the agony, courage, and cynical humor of Berenice. Frankie wins neither of her conflicting goals—to become perfectly joined and to become independent. Similarly, Berenice cannot find Ludie alive and become a member again of that perfect wedding, nor can she "bust free." She settles for a life with T. T. Williams, which promises a measure of congeniality and of independence. Frankie cannot go with Jarvis and Janice and be perfectly joined, nor can she become perfectly free by running away from home. She also settles for compromise with a new friend and a new school, but in giving up the past, she seems coldly to give up her affection for John Henry and Berenice and her wildest imaginings and aspirations. If the book maintains its "precision" to the end, it can hardly present the characters achieving harmony, because their hopes are too contradictory to be reconciled. Or perhaps Carson McCullers is saying that in this imperfect world the adult not only has to settle for the second-best but that he is, in a sense, morally obliged to do so.

CHAPTER 6

Clock Without Hands *(1961)*

I   *"A Worker of Miracles" or a Diminishing Artist?*

FIFTEEN years elapsed between *The Member of the Wedding* and Carson McCullers' fifth and final novel, *Clock Without Hands* (1961). Her illnesses, her husband's suicide, her mother's death, and her deep depression following the failure on Broadway of *The Square Root of Wonderful* (1958) must have contributed to the preoccupation with death which pervades this book, on which she worked for ten years.[1] In it, a half dozen deaths occur in a little over a year in 1953 and 1954 in the town of Milan, Georgia, where five other people had died in a short period eighteen years before. The earlier deaths inform McCullers' vision and intensify the brooding, somber effect generated in the novel. Two women die in childbirth, and two people slowly succumb to cancer. Violent deaths in both periods reflect racial conflict: a black man murders a white and is executed; a retarded black adolescent dies when a policeman carelessly strikes him; a black youth hangs the pet dog of a white youth and he himself is later killed when his house is bombed by racists.

The critical reaction to this book in the year following its appearance is remarkable. At least forty essays and substantial reviews appeared within a year, many by notable critics and authors. They appeared widely in popular magazines, scholarly journals, and all major newspapers. More remarkable than the quantity of reviews is their range of judgment about the quality of the novel and the intensity with which these judgments are expressed.

While writers on McCullers since her death express disappointment in the stereotypical nature of the embittered young black, Sherman Pew, such was not the case in early reactions. Nick

Aaron Ford, for instance, reviewing books published in 1961 which examined the theme of black identity, chose *Clock Without Hands* as "the most significant novel of the year concerning race relations."[2] To him, it was "moral, without preachment"; and he perceived that Jester Clane and Sherman Pew must not be viewed as realistic Georgia teenagers but as figures representing contemporary youth, black and white. Their meetings he interpreted as symbolic fantasy in which blacks reject white liberals, because they cannot yet understand one another.

Gore Vidal termed the novel a "near-failure" because McCullers, whose vision had always been "intensely private," threw her work "a little out of kilter" by pursuing a public issue in this novel. Nevertheless, while many others noted a loss in her usual brilliant virtuosity of language, Vidal declared her prose to be "one of the few satisfying achievements of our second-rate culture," and he sweepingly predicted that "of all the Southern writers, she is the most likely to endure."[3] Charles Rolo in *Atlantic*, recognizing the book's "impeccable craftsmanship" and the richness of its "wry comedy," declared it a strong contender for the National Book Award for fiction.[4] Tennessee Williams affirmed his friend as "a worker of miracles" and "the greatest living writer of our country, if not of the world."[5]

Positive reviews tended generally to praise the novel but to find it less good than one or more of McCullers' earlier works. The most common weaknesses mentioned were a lack of controlled organization, a carelessness in style, or a dependence on flat or stereotypical characterization. Several concluded that McCullers at less than her best was still one of the most interesting of American writers. At least two extreme reviews—reminiscent of reactions to *Reflections in a Golden Eye* twenty years earlier—denounced the book as exemplifying a general trend toward moral decadence in fiction.[6]

The range and complexity of disagreement and the strongly emotional tone of the reviewers—ranging from disappointment and anger to excitement, enthusiasm, and even joy—cannot be explained by study of the book alone. They surely reflect the facts that McCullers' early work had made an unforgettable impression on thousands of readers, that she had written no novel for fifteen years, that her recent attempt at drama had failed, and that no critic could be unaware that she, like her main character, J. T. Malone, faced death.

The social and intellectual climate of the early 1960s must also be considered in evaluating the outpouring of critical response to

Clock Without Hands. That the book remained one of the top ten best-sellers for many months indicates, perhaps, that between the time which the book ostensibly elucidates (1953 - 54) and when it was published (1961), racism had become fully recognized as a national and international problem and also as one which reached back to the beginning of history. McCullers' social satire presented the milieu of 1953 and 1954 with a comic detachment and a bitter nostalgia to which readers in 1961 could respond. The incidents of racial violence, ironically stylized to exaggerate the impassiveness of white bystanders and curiosity-seekers, would, in 1961 in any part of the United States, have produced riots.

Apart from the revival of interest in a famous author who had been silent for some years and apart from the cultural climate in which the book first appeared, one must, in speculating upon the widely differing responses of early critics, consider above all the unusual and ambitious artistic aims of Carson McCullers in her last book. Her aspirations were exciting in scope but were hardly possible for any author to achieve fully. That she attempted so much makes her book of consequence in literary history; that she so largely succeeded in doing so, surprised and impressed many. Certainly she gambled audaciously in her attempt to bring together, often with deliberately abrupt transitions, the realistic portrayal of a historical political situation and symbolic fantasy; to bring together repeatedly a violent tragedy and a sequence of broadly satiric comedy; to bring together flat stereotypical figures like the Judge and a deeply understood character like J. T. Malone; and to pursue throughout an entire novel two sets of largely unrelated themes— those involving the individual's facing of death and those involving racial conflict and abuse of political and legal power. Though this novel aroused great interest when it appeared, critics since that time have too readily dismissed it. More than most of McCullers' fiction, it now stands in need of new reading, interpretation, and evaluation.

II   *Chronological versus Psychological Measuring of Time*

In *Clock Without Hands* Carson McCullers most closely identifies with the point of view of J. T. Malone, the town druggist, as she traces his gradual dying and his philosophical and psychological reaction to his fate. Malone learns in the opening pages that he has leukemia; fifteen months later, as the book closes, he dies at the age of forty-two. The precise hour of his death he can never ascertain; consequently, he lives his life according to a clock without hands.

An inept elderly politician, who is completely without vision, Judge Fox Clane, also lives according to a clock without hands, because he attempts to ignore the course of history and the passage of time. He considers it a compliment to be called a reactionary who would turn back the clock a hundred years. Presented as a stereotypical and comic figure, the corpulent Judge plans continually to outwit death, as he has just done in recovering from a stroke. He scoffs at the prognosis that Malone's doctor has given, because he himself has never heard of leucocytes; therefore, they cannot be important. He tries to monopolize his two eighteen-year-old companions: his orphaned grandson, Jester Clane, who has lived with him since birth, and his employee, a blue-eyed Negro, Sherman Pew, who administers his insulin shots and who writes his letters to congressmen to persuade them to restore monetary value to Confederate currency. When Pew reads Dickens to the Judge, the sentimental eighty-five-year-old man sobs aloud "over orphans, chimney sweeps, stepfathers, and all such horrors" (134),[7] but he himself shows no concern for the more immediate difficulties of Jester, Sherman Pew, or Verily, his servant of fifteen years.

The Judge nostalgically mourns for the Old South, and even more for a personal world that was shattered eighteen years earlier when his wife, Miss Missy, died of cancer. Her death occurred shortly after the violent demise of their only son, Johnny, an attorney, who shot himself on Christmas Day. Soon after the suicide, Johnny's wife also died, giving birth to Jester. Jester's name is, indeed, an ironic one for a child born into a household where so much grief prevailed. At about that time, another fateful event occurred. The townspeople discovered a blue-eyed black foundling in a church pew, and immediately concluded that it must be the son of Sherman Jones, a black man recently executed for the murder of a white man, Ossie Little, during a quarrel over the latter's wife. The community named the mulatto baby *Sherman Pew*, as if to recognize both the supposed father and the place of the baby's discovery.

Jester and Sherman are closely linked, however, because Johnny Clane loved the mothers of both, because he unsuccessfully defended Sherman's father, and because Judge Clane pronounced Jones's death sentence. Nevertheless, the youths are eighteen before they learn what has been common gossip in the town for many years and before they learn the full extent of the Judge's misuse of power and his cruelty to those—even in his family—who disagree with him. Johnny Clane confided to the Judge a few days before his suicide that Mrs. Little, whom he had hopelessly loved, had called him to her bedside as she lay dying, after bearing the son of her black lover, and had bitterly reviled him because his defense of Sherman Jones had not saved him.

Eighteen years after he pronounced the sentence, Judge Clane still defends his decision. He tells Jester that, in sentencing blacks for crimes against whites, he depends less on the evidence presented than on his passion to preserve the "heritage of the South," a euphemism for white supremacy. According to the Judge, passion, which is often rooted in racial pride, is more important than legality or rationality. Such passion for one's region and race and such bigotry constitute for the Judge the most sublime evidence of manhood and patriotic devotion.

The Judge always reckons without thought of human nature as such, particularly with black individuals, and has little intimation of how the truth about Sherman's parentage will inflame the ordinarily passive and arrogant youth. Pew discovers the facts as he files papers in the Judge's office. He had assumed that his mother was still alive and was perhaps a famous black woman. In order to avoid acknowledgment of any significant linkage to the white race, he has chosen to account for his blue eyes by imagining that his father was a white rapist whose identity could never be traced. The sudden discovery that his mother was white, an adultress who died at his birth, and that his father was a black man executed for the murder of her husband shocks and troubles the youth profoundly. His bitterness increases as he learns of the involvement of Johnny Clane and the Judge in his father's trial. Enraged at what he considers the wrongs done him before his birth, he tries to retaliate by the symbolic gesture of hanging a pet dog that belongs to Jester, the only person who has ever gone out of his way to befriend him. Jester remains unbelievably patient—perhaps masochistic—in his attempts to secure Pew's friendship, in spite of the continual insults heaped upon him.

Violence and death are the chief concomitants of Sherman Pew's endeavors to attain higher social status. When he moves into an all-white neighborhood, buys a grand piano, and plans a lavish reception, Jester warns him of a racist plot against him. He goes ahead with the plans and is triumphantly playing the piano when Sammy

Lank, a poor laborer, throws a bomb in at the window and blows him to bits.

Out of his great devotion to his friend, Jester plans immediate vengeance. To achieve his design, he takes Sammy Lank for a ride in his plane and intends to shoot him when they are above the clouds. At the last minute, Jester recognizes in a sudden revelation that his vengeful passion derives from the same bitter feelings which motivate a mob when its members engage in lynchings. Jester now sees that he, like the Judge, is attempting to act on a purely personal ethos, which seems most quickly responsive to a situation, instead of depending on deliberative legal justice. He begins to understand that his zeal to avenge the death of Sherman Pew may be no different from the Judge's bigotry. During the plane ride when Sammy Lank tells the story of his pointless and frustrating life, Jester is overwhelmed by the recognition that Sammy is, no less than Sherman Pew or perhaps himself, a victim of circumstance. Circumstance has made of Sammy an unwitting clown, as well as a man without hope. After his wife's first pregnancy culminated in the delivery of "three younguns and two things" (232), Sammy aspired to become a famous man by fathering quintuplets. Fourteen children, among them twins and triplets, now burden him. A framed news clipping on his living room wall announces the birth of the triplets, his sole claim to the attention of others before he volunteers to throw the bomb.

Not knowing whether to laugh or to cry at the absurdity and futility of Sammy's story, Jester finds his anger spent. He circles back to earth without killing the naive and childlike man. If Jester's impulse to kill Lank is irrational, his decision not to do so is also prompted by unexplainable feelings and perhaps by some recognition that murdering another man would be uncivilized and a source of revulsion to his real self. Modern society itself, he realizes, is oppresive and misdirected, if a man such as Sammy must be associated with sensational births or with a violent crime in order to secure attention.

The novel closes on May 17, 1954, the day the Supreme Court decrees the end of segregation in public schools. Judge Clane appears to have suffered another stroke as a result of his rage when he realizes the full import of the news dispatch. He rushes to the local radio station to broadcast his protest. On this same spring afternoon, J. T. Malone willingly dies, after long months of rebellion and anger at his fate. He is conscious of his old friend's voice coming from the bedroom radio, but responds neither to the magnitude of the court action nor to the foolishness of the Judge's performance. In death, he is beyond such mundane matters. To Judge Clane, this day marks the death of the South, because the white race has lost incontrovertible power over the black race. Slipping into senility, he mindlessly recites the Gettysburg address. The Judge, still living according to a clock without hands, chooses not to recognize that the world has changed in the almost "four score and seven years" since his birth.

Although McCullers began this novel in 1951, she published it in 1961, seven years after the momentous 1954 Supreme Court decree, which provides the background for her closing scene. If these dates are crucial in understanding the critical and public response to the novel when it appeared, they are also crucial in interpreting McCullers' ironic intent and the implications of the comic social satire throughout the novel. If the Judge appears anachronistic in 1954, the other characters are, in varying degrees, more awkwardly out of step with the times by 1961.

In recalling the day of the court decision from the remoteness of seven years, McCullers, with modulated irony, implies that this day was not the turning point the Judge understood it to be. The foolish Judge, who thinks the clock of the South is tolling midnight, was wrong, but the people who thought the clock marked a new dawn because of this decision were just as wrong. The clock that monitors social progress is almost always without hands. The Judge, to the extent that he symbolizes bigotry and misuse of power, outwits death once more. The liberal attorney, Johnny Clane, who bungled the legal cause for the black and who died of the scorn provoked by his effort and by his failure, has been able only to inspire his son, who is also a well-intentioned bungler, to reach out to the oppressed blacks. For his son, Jester, more hope exists, but McCullers carefully shows that Jester is drawn to espouse the cause of racial justice by motives that are suspect—a vague and sentimentalized guilt assumed merely because he was born white, a juvenile curiosity about racial differences, and the personal satisfaction to be achieved in rescuing or avenging a black. Only at the close of the book does Jester begin to recognize the complexity of the human and economic issues he faces.

Sherman Pew's anger held no promise for himself or for the South as one looks back from 1961. The protest of Verily, who quits working for the Judge because he will not pay the employer's contribution to her Federal Social Security, is of more consequence than Sherman's suicidal gesture in moving into an all-white neighborhood and planning a party at which he will serve champagne and caviar, although he has never tasted them. Bitter and reckless, he separates himself from blacks as well as from whites. Though he despises the Judge, he takes notes on his vocabulary so that he can talk like him. His unworthy ambitions for higher status are fired by superficial commercial appeals—he buys Calvert whiskey and Hathaway shirts because of "man of distinction" advertising, aimed at status-seeking whites. A too-precipitous rate of social change in the early civil rights movement disoriented young blacks as well as whites and frustrated their attempts to obtain justice for themselves. (The fact that Sherman is a blue-eyed mulatto may be a symbolic indication of his confusion in his search for racial and personal identity. This mixture of physical characteristics does not symbolically join the races, as Berenice's glass blue eye seems to in *The Member of the Wedding.*)

In 1961 McCullers' cynicism about the progress on civil rights in the South and elsewhere went far beyond her simple denunciations of the Judge, who represents the bigotry of the Southern past and of the conservative elderly. Prejudice and violence did not die in 1954 in those old politicians of whom the Judge is representative. Prejudice and violence, furthermore, appeared to be on the upsurge in younger Southerners. Blacks like Sherman Pew were alienated from other blacks as well as from whites. Struggling white laborers, like Sammy Lank, felt increasingly threatened by integration in housing and employment.

Though Jester, as a liberal white youth, represents the hope of the South, McCullers presents this hope as only a tentative one. He is still immature, protected, bewildered—a "jester," a fool with occasional flashes of insight hidden from political strategists. He has learned much from his fascination for Sherman Pew, from his distress over the death of the retarded black adolescent called Grown Boy, and from his plane ride with the murderer, Sammy Lank. Nevertheless, he remains an awkward youth, whose talk is stilted and naive and who is more impulsive than thoughtful. In him, we hear too often the petulant unreasoned voice of twelve-year-old Paris Lovejoy in *The Square Root of Wonderful*, the play that McCullers wrote during the early years of her work on *Clock*

Without Hands. Jester is not, however, the object of McCullers' disdain as is Paris, and he exhibits generally a fuller development as an individualized, if lonely and eccentric youth.

In his most convincing scene, Jester recognizes, as he looks down from the descending plane, that the apparent orderliness of the landscape represents "an order foreign to the heart" (233) and that the community traces a harmonious and exact design only if the viewer is physically miles above it in a plane or spiritually distant, securely placed high up in the hierarchical social order of the South. To understand the South as it really is, one must renounce theories, abstractions, and prejudices and see the people for what they are, rather than view them from a physical or psychic distance. One must circle back down to the "secret corners of the sad backyards" and "look long into the eyes" of individuals (234), to see the traditions of the region for the ossified conventions that they really are.

But McCullers' social satire directed at racism, extreme conservatism, and parochialism, though notable, is not finally the most memorable aspect of this novel. Her central focus, from the first, is on the mystery of death, a state opposite, but inseparable from, life as J. T. Malone confronts his own end. To suggest how closely interwoven are the threads of life and death, McCullers stressed, as a parallel to Malone's struggle toward death, the struggle of Jester Clane to adjust to a widening vision as he approaches adulthood, to explore the intricacies of human relationships, and to recognize his own limitations and ambitions. Jester is, at times, a character flexible and complex enough to bridge the two plots in the book—the satirical plot with its social orientation and the main plot with its focus on the timeless theme of death. As a symbolic figure representing liberal white youth, Jester is never a realistic adolescent, but neither is he a flatly comic stereotype like the Judge—or even as flat a character as Sherman Pew. Jester's motivations and conflicts frequently baffle himself as much as they surprise the reader.

The questions which Malone and Jester, the two fully developed figures in the novel, must confront have no beginning nor end and they must, therefore, be measured by a clock without hands. If the clock that measures social change hides from even these thoughtful characters any assurance of progress, the social and local manifestations of these questions and conflicts cannot be evaded for that reason.

Unlike McCullers' earlier speculations in fiction about time and its meaning in establishing human identity, as in Frankie's troubled meditations in *The Member of the Wedding*, time here relates clearly to social change in the region. The Southerner—young or old, black or white—by 1953 can no longer predict his life in terms of the stability engendered by social convention, by tradition, or by the settled expectations of his class or his race. By the book's publication in 1961, social change related to race and class had so greatly accelerated and respect for repressive traditions of all kinds had so greatly diminished that individual limitations on social and financial success, as well as on personal freedom and fulfillment, were less accurately predictable on the basis of the race or class or region of one's birth.

III   *A Preoccupation with Death and with Death-in-Life*

In J. T. Malone's progress toward death, McCullers dramatizes her most obsessive theme in this novel: Though death is inevitable and universal, the process of dying is a uniquely individual experience. Malone's slow death also exemplifies a crucial subsidiary theme: As individuals die, they become in American society inevitably isolated, because people around them refuse to acknowledge the reality of death and so will not discuss it. Like most of the isolated people in McCullers' novels, then, Malone regards himself as a misfit. In his case, it is precisely his dying which sets him apart.

McCullers reveals herself throughout this sequence as conscious of the fundamental ironies in Malone's situation, ironies which derive in large part from the limitations of human nature itself, rather than from the malice of any individual. Since men and women tend by nature to be evasive whenever a strong positive emotional reaction is demanded of them, they often regard a dying individual as abnormal, even while they forget that they, too, will all die. Malone lives "surrounded by a zone of loneliness" (8), because he is at present so much more vulnerable to death than his associates and so something of a freak as far as they are concerned. They refuse to see in him a representative of the universal forces to which they must also succumb. Malone generates their hostility—as in the doctor's fumbling with the sharp letter-opener when he breaks the bad news to Malone in the first scene—whereas, he ought to engage their curiosity and their sympathy.

Another ironic paradox inheres in the situation that death for some people, in direct contrast to Malone's own, provides the only

source of possible attention that they ever receive from the community. Instead of a newly-imposed isolation, these people attain,
for once, a visibility to others. For example, Grown Boy achieves a
brief prominence because of the violence surrounding his end, not
because of his long tragedy as a handicapped child. The social tensions arising from his dying make him momentarily of significance
to a public who will, however, soon forget him.

A further irony subsists in McCullers' view that tragedy most
fully inheres in the limited and deprived aspect of a person's ordinary existence rather than in his death. McCullers not only introduces this theme when the decent, yet undistinguished, Malone
hears that he is soon to die, but she also reiterates it, often by implication, in the fates of several of her other characters. In this book
a number of individuals die before they can discover meaning in
their lives and solace in human relationships. The dullness,
barrenness and limitations of their daily experience make living for
such people inconsequential and their dying is equally pointless.

Not only do Sherman Pew and Sammy Lank embody this theme
of wasted human potential, but so do the retarded adolescent
Grown Boy and the blind and legless black beggar, Wagon, so-
called because he must be transported in a child's coaster wagon.
Grown Boy waits all week for Sunday, simply because the Judge
gives him a dime on his way home from church when he stops at
Malone's drugstore for a drink. Wagon's life is even more deadened, depressed, and demeaning. His name designates something
which is no part of himself—he is named in recognition of what is
missing or amputated. He does not even have artificial legs to substitute for that which has made him different from others; he survives through the use of his wagon, ordinarily a child's plaything.

As senseless as the fact that he was born with a mental defect, is
the incident which brings Grown Boy's death. McCullers does not
present suffering as a force which makes the victim saintly. Bitter
and mean from his struggles, Wagon enjoys a piece of chicken and
stingily refuses the boy a bite. Grown Boy spits on the food, grabs a
few coins from the beggar's cup, and runs. Jester, in the ensuing
outcry, catches Grown Boy, whom he has known all his life because
he is Verily's nephew. The policeman takes him from Jester's arms;
carelessly cracks his head with his nightstick; and the boy is dead.
His death is as sudden as that of Sherman Pew, whose murder it
presages. If the bystanders dismiss Grown Boy's death because they

are white and he is black, Pew, though black, dismisses it because he always "was just a feeb" (105). But Verily expresses the profound, impassioned grief which McCullers saw in the lives of the handicapped. Verily throws her apron over her head and sobs loudly: "And in all these years he never had his share of sense" (111).

It is the deaths of these people who have not yet had their "share" of life that disturb the reader. McCullers may present her abnormal or eccentric figures with some comic verve, but the barren quality of their lives always weighs heavily on her mind. In this novel, the tragedy of their deaths increases precisely because their lives have been so pointless. For them, the clock has never had hands, because their lives are too insignificant to be the subject of any sort of measurement. Each day for them is a repetition of every other day, full of hopeless monotony. The moment of their death will matter just a little, for the negative aspects of their lives comprise the real tragedy.

If Malone's life has, in fact, been less bleak than the lives of some of the others (Grown Boy, Wagon, Sammy Lank, Sherman Pew, and the child-bride who later became the mother of Sherman Pew) he, nevertheless, feels wronged by life. His passage through life has been uneventful, though it may have been more meaningful than he can credit it as being. In fact, he may have cheated himself by his failure to react intensely to the experiences that he has had. He attaches little value to daily existence until he hears that he is about to die, because previously he had been content to be passive and phlegmatic. Bitterly he realizes that he has, without knowing it, already died as a person possessing sensitivity, imagination, and individuality. He has lived by convention and has indeed been crushed by it, much as the pestle he uses in his pharmacy crushes the medications that he prepares. When he cannot bear to think of death, he turns to the equally depressing exploration of "the tedious labyrinth of his life" (148). He wonders now "how he could die, since he had not yet lived" (150). Unimportant as Malone appears to be, he is an everyman figure in the sense that he represents what the average individual can become if he loses his freshness of spirit. Death is no less mysterious and fearsome when it comes to the ordinary individual than when it cuts down the greatly heroic, noble, or powerful.

IV   *"Death Is Always the Same,*
but Each Man Dies in His Own Way"

Carson McCullers recognized that those who know they are
about to die move through roughly recognizable stages of
awareness, rebellion, and finally acceptance. She realized also that
dying differs for each person and that is successive phases need
not be clearly defined. Nor do the dying traverse these plateaus of
philosophical understanding and psychological and physical adjustment in any predictable order or in any predictable period of time.
The process of dying is a turbulent one, and the victories of courage
or faith achieved by any individual on any day may yield to fear or
petulance the next day or even the next minute. A change in the
weather, an overheard comment, a touch, or an odor can cause the
dying person to react excessively or can produce no effect on him at
all. For the moment, he loves life intensely, hates it beyond reason,
or feels apathy concerning it. If the dying individual disturbs those
around him, who expect him to be more rational than he can be in
this "zone of loneliness," he is himself confused by his unpredictable anger, fear, and grief.

When Malone hears of his impending death in the opening pages
of the book, he responds with humility and embarrassment, as if he
had failed a test and as if the doctor's judgment had humiliated
him, as his failing in medical school had. Though he is an essentially
honorable man, he seems never to have felt worthy even of the little
that life has yielded him. When the doctor breaks to him the news
of his fatal illness, Malone resents the physician's nervous, shifting
gaze and interprets his behavior as a reflection upon his own un-
worthiness. When tears appear in Malone's eyes for a moment, he
immediately apologizes for them, as if his own death should be of
no consequence even to himself. On the examining table he is
ashamed of his thin body. Later he focuses on his knobby feet as the
part of his body that he most loathes, and he hastens to cover them
with his stockings to hide their ugliness. The irony strikes him that
it is this hated body, of which he is ashamed, that has kept him alive
and that will soon cause him to cease to exist.

After his initial disbelief and anger and after he achieves some
perspective on his situation, Malone begins to search for some
philosophical significance in his oncoming death. He hopes first for
a confirmation of the possibility for personal immortality and for an
assurance that some relationship exists between living a decent life

on earth and enjoying a reward in heaven. But he finds that a reasoned view on these ultimate questions is difficult to attain. The superficiality of the "upbeat" Baptist preacher in his sermon "Salvation Draws a Bead on Death" and the man's uneasy evasiveness when Malone talks with him discourage him. Discouraging also is the Judge's denial that his illness can be serious and, conversely, his wife's immediate acceptance of the doctor's prognosis as fact. Without taking time to rebel against his doom and her approaching widowhood, Ellen Malone too quickly tries to cheer him, to recall nostalgically the years of their marriage, and to make the most of the life that is left. It is months before Malone is ready to accept her ministry of comfort and her quiet planning for the continued life of the family after his death. He knows that she accepts his death too readily and too complacently, since it is an experience that she herself is not undergoing.

In the days immediately after he learns of his illness, Malone is shocked by "all the life he had spent unlived" (150). He torments himself with thoughts of women he might have loved, winter vacations in Maine or Vermont he might have taken, and his frustrated hope of becoming a physician rather than a pharmacist. In a surge of life, he plants a garden, but then forgets it. Aware of the years he has wasted, he now becomes fanatical about the minutes or the seconds that he may lose, and he fusses with the jeweler about the improper adjustment of his watch, as if to indicate his own obsession with the passing of time. When enough time has gone by, he will, of course, be dead.

Malone realizes that he is dying in body in these months, but is startled to realize that he has, to a marked degree, already died in spirit. He cannot recall the point at which his love for his wife, his pleasure in his work, his strong sexuality, and his pride in his family lessened. By autumn, he grimly contemplates the emptiness and insensitivity of his spirit in the past and relates it to the mocking sound of the woodpecker pecking a hollow pole in the November twilight and to the "brassy clamor of the city clock, uncadenced and flat" (157). Dazed by excessive fatigue, he wonders when it was that his "self" had slipped away.

In this book McCullers develops constantly the concept that life and death are not polarities but the extremes on a continuum, where most people exist closer to a state of deadness than to a state in which they would be fully alive. In tracing the philosophical and psychological changes in Malone, she skillfully suggests the intensity, the dullness, or the absence of sensory perception as she portrays the relative presence or absence of human vitality. Malone himself is frightened whenever he tries to imagine a state of nonexistence, and he finds the thought hypnotic or paralyzing in its effect.

As he contrasts the living and the dying, he recalls the sad days when Miss Missy was dying and he would in the evening deliver opiates to the Clane mansion. To hide the reason for his errand, he would take a few flowers from his garden or a bottle of perfume from his store and leave these for the woman who would, ironically, be unable to see the flowers or to smell the perfume because her body would be continuously deadened by the drugs.

The irony of such contrast between living and dying haunts him again when he returns from visiting the Judge late one night, and is aware of his own worsening disease as Miss Missy had been aware of hers. He slips into bed, having evaded his wife's encouragement to greater sexual intimacy than they had known for several years. He is agonized by brushing against her body, because her sexual vitality contrasts with his fatigue and brings to him a great sense of loss and listlessness.

McCullers refuses to be sentimental in her depiction of the dying Malone. Suffering does not make him virtuous, kindly, gentle, or patient. He grows irritable, petty, jealous of anyone who is in good health, and particularly resentful of his wife, with her loving attentions and her invitations to renew the sexuality of their earlier married life. Morbidly he seeks out the details of every death he hears about, whether or not he even knew the person who has died. Only the fact of their dying, not the consequences of their living, makes these people important to him. When he goes to his younger brother's funeral, the rouge on the cheeks of the corpse preoccupies him more than does his grief for his brother.

By the time Malone dies in May 1954, he has mellowed. He is no longer disturbed that the moment after death his body will be a corpse; nor is he anxious about heaven and hell and his relationship to these concepts. He thinks now only of Ellen's questions about the desired warmth of the hot-water bottle at his feet and whether or not he wants ice in his drink as she ministers to his immediate comfort. He dies before she returns from the kitchen with the glass of cold water, but it does not matter. Malone never did have all that he hoped for in his ordinary life.

V   *Malone, the Judge, and Jester: Organizing Entities in the Novel*

Basic as Malone's death is to the thematic line of *Clock Without Hands*, his presence throughout the novel contributes significantly to its aesthetic effects and structural design. He, rather than Judge Clane, provides the strong emotional center in the novel. His inevitable progress toward an unspecified moment of death, like the changing of the seasons, provides the author with a definite, but somewhat flexible, measure of the passing of time. Because Malone witnesses, or comments upon, most of the situations and characters in the novel—as well as the momentous events which occurred eighteen years earlier—he provides the work with a degree of unity. As a middle-aged man, he becomes a pivotal figure between the outmoded political and social views of the elderly Judge Clane and the immature views and impulsive behavior of the adolescents, Jester Clane and Sherman Pew. A relatively inarticulate person, Malone continually supplements with his silent musings the voice of the narrator and extends the range of the authorial comment by thus indicating his own point of view. Malone's views on others cannot always be accepted as reliable, because they may reveal more of his anger, his frustration, or his lethargy at a particular stage in his dying than they reveal of the truth about others.

If Malone, thus, provides philosophical balance and structural unity and extends the view of the narrator, Jester Clane similarly figures in the orderly overall design of the work, largely through McCullers' "pairing" him with other figures. He contrasts with his grandfather in age and in his liberal views on racial integration and politics. He parallels Sherman Pew as a youth of similar age, as a person who bows to the Judge's authority and who is responsible to the Judge for financial support, while rejecting his views. Jester Clane's dream is to perform a solo flight in his plane, and he attains the dream; Sherman Pew's dream is to play his grand piano in his own house, and he also attains his dream. The two are paired in the tragic circumstances that surrounded the year of their birth and in their independent but almost simultaneous discovery of these long-kept secrets. Jester also parallels his father, Johnny Clane, as the pride of the Judge's life and as the source of his greatest anger and disappointment. Like his counterpart, Johnny, Jester reaches out to help blacks, and, like him, he muddles the situations that he seeks to rectify. Johnny cannot prevent the execution of Sherman Jones;

Jester facilitates, unwittingly, the death of Grown Boy and fails also to prevent the killing of Sherman Pew, although he knows of the plot against him.

Perhaps the most significant key to the structure and design of this novel is the stereotypical portrayal of Judge Clane, who is so artificial that the ironic tone of the political satire remains consistent. A degree of artistic tension exists, as a result, between McCullers' comic attack on racism and conservatism embodied in the Judge and her poignant treatment of the other themes, related to death. Those who in the last ten years have seen this novel as evidence of McCullers' loss of artistry in her late career primarily criticize her creation of the flat and stereotypical Judge Clane. Had he been less clearly a caricature, however, the political satire would have become too insistent and portentous, and thereby detracted from McCullers' probing of the mysteries of death. The farcical comedy—most broadly contrived in the absurd "murder" of the Judge, who simply refuses to notice that he has been "killed" by Sherman Pew's injecting water instead of insulin in his veins for three days—would not have registered so incisively had the Judge's humanity been more fully established. Pew must finally shrug his shoulders on the fourth day and admit that the Judge and what he symbolizes is too strong for an assassination attempt. This comic treatment of what Pew visualizes as political murder provides an ironic contrast to the later hanging by Pew of Jester's dog and to the melodramatic conspiracy which culminates in Pew's own death. In that contrived event, the Judge foolishly insists that *everyone* should take part in the killing of Sherman so that *no one* will be guilty. In a final mockery of human beneficence, the Judge pays the mortician for disposing of Sherman Pew with propriety. With the Judge present, there can be no thought of sincere grief—only the coldest of satirical comedy.

The flatness of the Judge's anachronistic portrayal contrasts strikingly with the ambience which enriches McCullers' use of factual history in an exact time and place, with her probing of human identity in the figures of Malone and Jester, and with her portrayal of the ordinary individual's struggles with fear, anger, loneliness, and grief. Only a writer possessing McCullers' audacity would have featured a figure with a Ku Klux Klan mentality to comment upon the blacks and their civil rights in Georgia in the explosive years of 1953 and 1954. The Judge must necessarily remain a caricature. Even when he is seen occasionally as a confused old man left behind by a changing South, McCullers in this more sympathetic light never allows his gentility, chivalry, and nostalgia to excuse his stupidity and cruelty.

Evasiveness characterizes his very existence and all his ideas and values. Only he can take himself seriously; only he can look in the mirror at his 300-pound body and remark that he has always been portly but never stout. His grief for Miss Missy is associated with his sentimental enjoyment of melodramatic fiction; she becomes a symbol of romantic Southern womanhood for Clane ("a purer woman never lived" [52]). She could have been a woman loved for her own kindness, virtue, and humanity, as we can tell from Malone's remembrance of her grace. Clane's memories of her center on her superficial attributes, a fact McCullers treats lightly in her story of the Judge's brief search for a new wife.

Soon after Miss Missy's death, he began visiting all the churches in town to see whether any other woman's throat and breasts moved as beautifully when she sang in the choir as had Miss Missy's. Amused at his discreetness, McCullers makes clear that even a beautiful and pure woman who sang hymns would never have satisfied the Judge, unless she was, like Miss Missy, a good card player who enjoyed a drink with her husband. Because the Judge savors the dregs of old emotions, he is portrayed as not totally devoid of feeling. But his humanity is only residual; clearly, he is a fool, not a jester capable of insight and wisdom. He remains a ridiculous bigot and bully.

If the Judge consistently symbolizes racism and abuse of power, McCullers never dignifies him by making him an impressive or dramatic force of evil. He represents perhaps the worst kind of evil, a flabby, shallow kind, but his very complacency and lack of humanity make him more insidious than if he were "impressive." McCullers' comedy succeeds in keeping him a mere buffoon who sings in the bathtub, puts cologne behind each ear, and enjoys the routines of living, particularly those connected with his digestive system. So separate does McCullers keep her stylized political satire from her compelling treatment of the complexities of death that the Judge never realizes Malone is moving toward his end, although he was the first one to whom Malone confided the news of his doom. His obese body is to him still a fascinating possession, and he sees death as only something a person as sharp as he is outwits. The annoyance of dieting is the price a mortal pays grudgingly to beat death.

With Judge Clane as a measuring point, McCullers places her other characters—their words, attitudes, and behavior—in an appropriate satiric context. Everyone exists somewhere between common sense and absurdity, simply by his distance from, or proximity to, the Judge. In different scenes the same character can vary from the relatively foolish to the relatively wise through this means of placement. Whenever Malone, Jester, or Sherman are with the Judge, their dialogue becomes replete with social clichés and with slighting reference to the Jew or the "nigger." Jester, for example, is foolish and immature in all the scenes where he dines alone with the Judge. He is at his best when he is in his plane—as far away from the Judge as he can get. Verily is, for once, a positive character in the scene in which she quits her job and walks away from the Judge after fifteen years. Sherman Pew is bitter and insolent to the greatest degree when he is near the Judge, but he takes notes on the Judge's vocabulary so that he can be as pompous as the white man. Sherman's tall-tales about his adventures and distinction, which he swears to be the "real, actual," clearly relate to those the Judge tells about his own past glory as a statesman. Malone is at his worst when he allows the Judge and his cohorts to use the drugstore to plan their strategy against Sherman Pew.

McCullers did not complete the rigorous revision that might have produced greater tautness in her presentation of the conflict between the realistic and the human, on the one hand, with the artifices of satire, on the other. The bombastic speech and racist pride of old leaders (like the Judge), the violent rage of young blacks (like Sherman Pew), and the hostile competitiveness of low-income whites (like Sammy Lank) all suggest in their puppetlike movements the growing complexity of the problems of the South, although no attempt is made to analyze them adequately.

If the Supreme Court decree promises equal and integrated education, the decree is heard only as it is mediated through the senile babbling of a man who will try to live as if it were still "four score and seven years ago." McCullers refuses at every point in her presentation of the social and political South either to countenance an easy hope for better conditions in the future or to glorify the legendary past. No appropriate human horror or grief is evident after the bombing of Sherman Pew's house. She simply comments, about a matter completely irrelevant to this tragedy, "Mr. Peak who owned the grocery store adjoining the house had a very good business that night" (230). That so great a tragedy can be regarded with detachment and curiosity dehumanizes the community.

As Jester returns to earth in his plane, having decided against killing Sammy Lank, McCullers describes the way the rural landscape changes with the seasons in an orderly way, but she flatly discourages hope for orderly change in the towns that lie next to it: "the gray-green of cotton, the dense and spidery tobacco land, the burning green of corn. As you circle inward, the town itself becomes crazy and complex. . . . Gray fences, factories, the flat main street" (234).

McCullers, to a greater degree than in her earlier novels, focused in this last book upon the economic, political, and ideological aspects of the South as it was undergoing, or else resisting, change. Although she experimented with techniques of political satire, the exploiting of stereotype for ironic effect, and a stylized comedy of manners, her greatest talent remained where it had always been—in her dramatization of internal conflict in her characters. Racial antagonism, political controversy, class differences, and the barriers between generations are all issues explored in this novel, primarily as realities which magnify loneliness, isolation, and internal conflict.

Even in this final novel, then, Carson McCullers' emphasis remains upon the individual conflict, the solitary spirit of the human being, and the debilitating power of the Southern economy and social system to deny a sense of worth to the average individual—all themes dominant in her earlier works. If hope is to come to the South, it will come not through the orderly design, "foreign to the heart" (233), that one sees from a distance—from a plane, from the North, from the Judge's dim past, or from the world of political theorists. It must come through those who have wisdom to live down in the very midst of the region they would change and who will look long into the eyes of individual people and understand them in their own bleak backyards, perhaps better even than they can understand themselves.

The balance and symmetry, the inevitability of the action, and the naturalness of the dialogue of the best of McCullers' earlier fiction are all qualities, unfortunately, that are less evident in this last novel. Nevertheless, the precision that marked the height of McCullers' artistry in *The Ballad of the Sad Cafe* and *The Member of the Wedding* still occasionally appears as she evokes the intensity of a dramatic moment or as she sharply portrays a character through a single gesture, look, or exclamation. If the book is not consistently controlled and so lacks the highest degree of artistry, the poignancy and irony of certain events or words are impressive and suggest that the book might have become a master work.

CHAPTER 7

Short Stories, Poems, and a Second Play

I Stories of Childhood and Adolescence

A HALF-DOZEN of McCullers' published stories focus on a child or adolescent—of these, the most impressive attainment is "Wunderkind," her first published work, written when she was only fifteen, and "Correspondence," written in 1941, about the time of *The Ballad of the Sad Cafe*. While the six stories vary considerably in form and quality, McCullers analyzes in each the situation of a child caught in a difficult position and reacting to it with bewilderment and frustration. In each, the point of view is so clearly defined that the reader identifies completely with the child who is coping with the complexities both of his or her situation and the complexities of his or her own development as an individual.

One early sketch, "Breath from the Sky," commands attention for its presentation of a dying child entirely from that child's point of view and for its realism. The child is neither one who rejoices to see the gates of heaven opening nor one who blesses the family from whom she is departing. Constance, who appears to be dying of tuberculosis, feels that she is about to be abandoned by her family—and even by her hated, domineering nurse—as they prepare her for her trip to a rest home. Reclining in a chair on the lawn, she envies her family as they leave to go swimming, and she longs to be washed by the blue lake and to suck the blue sky into herself in order to make the color a part of her, thereby enlivening the dull gray of her existence. Unused to being out-of-doors, she focuses today on a blade of grass as she suffers a fit of coughing, because she has been used to focus on a crack in the floor in her room when she was caught by the coughing fits. She longs also for

117

the freshness of the sky, in order to escape the contamination she associates with her illness and which, she thinks, makes others reject her.

She is completely isolated and frustrated, because she feels that no one truly can sympathize with her. The efficient and cold nurse gives her admonitions about the value of cheerfulness. Her mother also makes every effort to appear unemotional, probably to keep from showing the child her own grief. Her voice is "brittle," and as she leaves, an almost imperceptible shudder passes across her shoulders. Constance interprets her mother's evasiveness as a rejection of her because of her "dirtiness."

Exhausted and loathing herself, Constance forces her mother to cut her long hair. So great is her sense of contamination that she will not let her sister even use the pile of hair to make a pillow for the dog. She tries not to spit out the thick strands of phlegm that drain from her lungs as she coughs. This central scene in which Constance demands that her hair be cut in an effort to be cleansed and accepted, becomes more poignant as one recognizes the energy with which the mother hacks at the girl's hair, as if determined to cut herself away from the child who must leave the next day—and possibly forever. Her hurrying away to take the rest of the family swimming may also suggest a determination on her part to keep the rest of the family involved in the satisfying routines related to life rather than death. The tension created by the mother's brittle voice and hurried movements and by the nurse's exaggerated cheeriness provides an ironic background for the child's thoughts about abandonment.

McCullers' portrayal contrasts with that of the archetypally innocent and serene dying child, so common in literature of the past and reaching its apogee in the death of Little Nell in Dickens' *The Old Curiosity Shop,* of Little Eva in Harriet Beecher Stowe's *Uncle Tom's Cabin,* and of Helen Burns in Charlotte Brontë's *Jane Eyre.* The use of the child's point of view, the realistic depiction of the ugliness of her disease, and the petulance, weariness, and self-loathing of the patient sweep aside any trace of sentimentality that one might associate with the death of a young person. Subtly, McCullers blends the child's longing to be clean and lovable with her disappointment in missing a chance to go swimming with the rest of the family. Because she writes from the child's perspective, McCullers convinces the reader that staying home from the swimming expedition and being sent away from her mother is worse than facing imminent death.

The forceful evocation of situation in this sketch elicits sympathy for the victim, although she is still a repugnant child and her disease is loathsome. Though it contains an arresting portrayal, "Breath from the Sky" is essentially static. It is a vignette, rather than a story in which the structure is well defined, in which tensions develop between individuals, and in which a character changes significantly. It is prophetic, however, in the sense that McCullers would actually become a distinguished creator of character, particularly of children.

In a more extended and dynamic portrayal of a troubled child, "The Haunted Boy" (1955), McCullers explores the trauma of ten-year-old Hugh, who returns from school to find his mother absent and then relives the experience which he has tried to forget. The previous year he had discovered his mother's bleeding body after she had attempted suicide, and he and his father had had to live alone for months after the mother was hospitalized. When Hugh's affectionate and lighthearted mother returns in an hour or so from her first shopping spree since her recovery, Hugh bitterly turns on her and tells her she looks too old for the frivolous dress and slippers she has bought. Through the reliving of his horror, through his expression of anger at his mother's willingness to abandon him and his father, and through the reassurance which both parents can now give him, Hugh by the end of the story gains a measure of peace. This work illustrates the psychic tension of a child torn between pity for—and anger against—a parent and also the tension between his need to appear mature and his need to express his fear. Most effective is the dramatic irony implicit in his sudden abusive anger at the very moment that he experiences relief at his mother's return.

In four other stories about young people, dramatic tension develops as each protagonist matures as a result of difficult and harrowing experience. "Sucker," "Like That," and "Wunderkind"preceded all of the novels; "Correspondence" followed *The Ballad of the Sad Cafe* in 1941. Primary interest in "Sucker" and "Like That" lies in their relation to McCullers' early development as artist, particularly her ability to depict character and her use of themes related to love and to the acquiring of self-knowledge. But "Wunderkind" and "Correspondence" deserve attention for their merit apart from their position in McCullers' canon.

In both "Sucker" and "Like That" McCullers analyzes parallel crises in the lives of two young siblings. The narrators, who are also the protagonists, plan simply to report facts about a brother or sister, but actually talk more about changes that have occurred in themselves as a formerly close relationship with a brother or sister has diminished. In "Sucker," sixteen-year-old Pete recounts how his twelve-year-old foster-brother has changed his name from "Sucker" to "Richard" after Pete one night, frustrated by Maybelle, his first love, angrily turned against Sucker. In "Like That" a thirteen-year-old talks about her older sister's preoccupation during the last several months with whatever had happened on "a certain night this summer" when she had stayed out late with a college student. In "Like That" the narrator is given no name and the sister is only called "Sis," perhaps to emphasize their representativeness as adolescents more than their individuality.

Pete's impatience with Sucker, followed by his remorse, anticipates Frankie Addams' ambivalent behavior toward little John Henry in *The Member of the Wedding*, as she alternately avoids him and then seeks his companionship; it also anticipates Mick Kelly's regret in *The Heart Is a Lonely Hunter* when Bubber changes his name to "George," becomes a "tough kid," and takes his best marbles out of their hiding place in her mattress.

Both protagonists communicate the satisfaction that they had experienced in the old days of spontaneous comradeship and recreate vividly the single eventful night that changed their relationship. For Pete, his guilt at hurting Sucker adds to the grief related to the child's separation from him. So does his chagrin when he realizes that loss of Sucker's admiration overshadows the frustration which he had felt over Maybelle's rejection of him, the event that led to the attack on Sucker. In "Like That," the narrator's bewilderment, her fears about her elder sister, and her apprehension that this same mysterious trouble may be her own fate in a few years' time deepen her sense of isolation and the pain of the psychic distance which now separates her from her sister.

Unfortunately, McCullers' effort in both of these stories to imitate the spontaneous language of the child or the adolescent results in loosesness of organization, relatively unconnected expressions of emotion, and the inclusion of irrelevant details. She had not yet developed the control of language and of action which she manifested in her novels and in some of her short stories. McCullers used first-person narration only one other time in her later fiction—in "Correspondence," in which the epistolary convention provides a degree of stylistic control. Her necessary mastery of the formal aspects of her artistry can be associated, in part, perhaps, with her abandonment of the first-person point of view and her subsequent use of an omniscient narrator.

In the better, though extremely early, "Wunderkind," McCullers demonstrates her ability to write with a more compressed and forceful style than she used in "Sucker" or "Like That." She reveals far greater control, directness, and economy in her depiction of fifteen-year-old Frances, who hopes to become a great pianist and who had, several years before, been hailed as a "Wunderkind" by the crotchety Mr. Bilderbach, her teacher. With no children of his own, he has projected his feeling toward her and has become for her a second father, just as his wife has become a mother of sorts to Frances, making her junior high graduation dress, for example, and providing milk and cookies when she comes twice a week for her lessons. For four months Frances has been discouraged because she cannot actualize the music that she hears in her mind and feels in her heart, although she has attained technical competence in the difficult compositions which she practices for hours each day. She does not understand the discrepancy between the music she hears in her mind and the music that she elicits from the piano, but she knows that she cannot stand the strain of this conflict much longer. All that seems real to her now is the music she hears in her mind and cannot duplicate when she sits down to play.

All the action, the dialogue—and most importantly, the music—filter through Frances' memory and reflect her anxiety. The story builds quickly to a climax and almost immediately ends. Frances arrives for the lesson late in the winter afternoon at the downtown Cincinnati apartment and rushes out a short time later as the story closes. Except for a brief encounter with the violinist who teaches Heime (another Wunderkind), only Frances and Bilderbach appear.

A maze of paradoxes surrounds Frances. The story would be far simpler—and less effective—if Bilderbach (or the more successful Heime) were her antagonist and she could direct her anger at him. Instead, the music, which is her greatest love, is also her antagonist. The music exists as part of herself, as well as an outside force to deal with. Bilderbach, though her judge on this crucial occasion, is also the only comrade she could depend on in her struggle with her overwhelming challenger. But even his comprehension of her situation is limited, and he also suffers from Frances' sense of defeat by music. She cannot return to the vigorous proficiency she had enjoyed in childhood any more than she can advance to the level of genius predicted by her teacher when she was only twelve. (When

Bilderbach, seeing the tears in her eyes, suggests she play a simple composition she knew three years before, she refuses.) Frances' abandoning of her music is not an impulsive yielding to discouragement, but rather an act of courage, because it represents her acknowledgment that a part of herself has died. As she leaves her teacher's apartment, music has vanished from the silent room and from her as a creative artist. Bilderbach stands mute, with hands relaxed and hanging at his side; and the door shuts firmly behind her. Every detail implies finality, that an essential part of Frances' self has gone.

The ending may suggest Frances' maturing—her realistic judgment of her ability and her facing of herself as a human being who struggles and still fails. More poignantly, however, the ending is devastating for Frances. Having made her decision after months of agonizing over her dilemma, she enjoys no elation or even relief. She stumbles, she drags her heavy books, and, once outside, she, ominously, turns in the wrong direction. The street's noise and confusion assail her senses. Ironically, the noise and confusion that intensify her suffering as she rushes down the street come from those happy children, who were never destined to be wonderful. She has lost her music and her special friends; beyond this, she realizes now that she earlier had lost irretrievably her life as an ordinary child, a life marked by noise, confusion, and laughter—and until now, she did not know that the loss of such experience mattered at all.

Though McCullers uses an impersonal narrative voice, she skillfully adapts the narrative passages to the child's feelings, particularly as Frances waits for her lesson to begin. She examines the picture of Heime on the cover of a music magazine and realizes that, though he has been the only child she has had time to associate with for three years because of her hours of practice, she actually does not know what he looks like. She knows exactly what his fingers look like when she performs at concerts with him, and she knows exactly what he smells like as he stands beside the piano. One recognizes from her thoughts on Heime the utter impersonality that has narrowed her life to a preoccupation with his fingers and with her own. She dismisses Heime from her mind with the thought: "Heime always seemed to smell of corduroy pants and the food he had eaten and rosin" (75).[1] As she looks at his picture, it occurs to her momentarily that "his finger looked as though it would pluck the wrong string" (71). But Heime is a mere distraction; music itself is her problem.

If she does not know what Heime looks like, we never know what she looks like because her appearance does not matter to her. We know how she moves—dragging her satchel, stumbling clumsily, and feeling her arms weighted down by her books. Her hands are enemies beyond her control: they fumble as she pulls out her music; her fingers twitch and her tendons quiver as she recalls her morning's practice; and she observes that the adhesive bandage on her sore finger is dirty and curling. As if the music she hears in her mind is the reality and what she actually hears is unreal because it is wrong, she looks intently at her fingers almost to reassure herself that they are part of her.

McCullers vividly creates the setting, the people, and the details found in the story, although we know Mrs. Bilderbach; Mr. Lafkowitz, the violin teacher; and Heime only through Frances' thoughts. The dialogue is sparse, occurring only at the most crucial points. When she finishes playing, for example, Mr. Bilderbach says only one word: "No." The single word changes her life. The precision and sensitivity revealed in this story, McCullers' first published work, provided sure evidence of her talent even before she left the South for New York.

In autumn 1941 McCullers wrote "Correspondence," an epistolary sketch in the voice of still another adolescent, fourteen-year-old Henrietta (Henky) Evans, who changes from an open and trusting young girl to a disappointed and cynical adult in her two and a half months of letter-writing to a South American boy who never answers, though he volunteered in a magazine to be a pen-pal. Henky declares, "Recently I have thought a whole lot about life. I have pondered over a great many things such as why we were put on the earth. I have decided that I do not believe in God. On the other hand, I am not an atheist" (MH, 154). Her letters suggest the one poignant truth about growing up—the attenuation of spontaneous emotion. Mistrust and suspicion in McCullers' work often mark the transition from childhood trustfulness to youthful experience. So in this story a guarded formality and a mere polite expression of disapproval replace in the fourth letter the appealing spontaneity of the first.

McCullers' artistic excellence may be most notable here in the subtlety with which she conveys what Henky herself does not realize—her self-centeredness. Though angry at Manoel's disinterest in her, she does not in her writing reach out to learn about a culture far different from her own. She remarks that she has always been "crazy about" South Americans, but has never met one. She would be disturbed if Manoel wrote and talked of himself and his land, rather than reacting to her letters. She seeks a mirror-image of herself in another hemisphere, just as the narcissistic characters in *The Heart Is a Lonely Hunter* talk to Singer, who seems to them to understand perfectly, although he, like Manoel, never answers. It is as if she writes the letters to herself, a kind of talking aloud.

Although her conclusions are pompous, Henky engagingly in the first letter acknowledges some of her shortcomings. She wants to be a tragic actress, but her performance in a recent play failed. Another failure, which anticipates the anxiety of Frankie Addams in *The Member of the Wedding*, lies in her inability to be "exactly like the other freshmen." She closes her first letter with the hope that Manoel's letter will arrive soon—to reassure her that he is the spiritual twin she seeks: "I am looking forward exceedingly to hearing from you and find out if I am right about our feeling so much alike about life and other things. You can write to me anything that you want to, as I have said before that I feel I already know you so well" (MH, 155).

The themes developed in Henky's letters are those encountered elsewhere in McCullers' fiction: the essential narcissism of human beings, the longing for reciprocity in any expression of interest or affection, and the ironic combination of gain and loss as one grows up. The sketch, however, deserves attention apart from its relationship to McCullers' explorations of these themes in her longer works. The humor in the treatment of the child is incisive, but McCullers tempers her satire of Henky's failure to recognize her self-centeredness with just the appropriate balance of the ironic and of good-natured tolerance.

II   *Humor in the Short Stories*

Besides "Correspondence," several other excellent stories reveal McCullers' satirical humor. Notable in her early work is the brief, single-scene story "The Jockey" (1941), which excels by virtue of its sustained tension between strong emotion and its repression. The whole situation explodes as emotions are let loose in the violent closing of the story. The story appeared in the *New Yorker* a month after McCullers completed it at Yaddo, just two miles from the Saratoga hotel where it is laid.

Against an elegant background in the hotel dining room, three rich men who derive fortunes from the racetrack sit stuffing themselves with rich food and drink. All regard the jockeys, who make their fortunes possible by risking their lives in the races, as less than human. They speak derisively of an older jockey, Bitsy Barlow, who has been "strange" ever since "his Irish friend" was killed three years before. Bitsy, they claim, has gained three pounds and still was seen eating a lamb chop.

Barlow enters the room. A tiny man, he exaggerates his impeccable manners with a haughty theatricality. He stands beside their table, condescendingly looking down on the men who figuratively look down on him and the other jockeys. With perfect control of his anger, he tells them the news of his young friend, injured months ago, whose cast was removed that morning and whose leg had shrunk. The three rich men remain unmoved by the news. With great aplomb, Bitsy astonishes them by deliberately removing two French fries from a plate, chewing them, and then spitting the food on the beautiful rug. He cries out loudly, "Libertines!" Immediately, he resumes his dignified bearing and marches rigidly from the room, leaving the startled trio to be humiliated by the curiosity and laughter of the other patrons in the dining room.

As memorable as the explosive climax is the hypnotic effect built from the beginning of the story by Barlow's cold and controlled hostility toward the three men, which continues to intensify until the moment of attack. Memorable also is the stylized artifice that balances the stereotypical rich men against the tiny figure who reveals compassion for the exploited and who protests against their exploitation. McCullers treats the three "libertines" only halfseriously, because they must not become fully human or appear as even an interesting subspecies. They must remain stereotypes, designated at first as the bookie, the trainer, and the rich man, and somewhat later merely as Sylvester, Simmons, and Seltzer.

The dramatic impact of the story largely derives from the contrast between Barlow's apparently impulsive act and the pride and dignity, the extreme restraint and propriety, and the precision and deliberateness which he has shown to the final moment. Impulse has no place in his world, where he must calculate each motion in order to pare from his time the few seconds by which he can set a new record in a race. McCullers also uses many details metaphorically to emphasize Barlow's characteristic rigidity: his heels bite sharply into the deep rug as he marches into the dining room; he bows stiffly; he combs his hair in a stiff band; he wears a "precisely" tailored suit; he opens his cigarette box with a definite snap; he sharply clinks his bracelet on the table; and he drinks his whiskey "neat in two hard swallows."

One might at first see Bitsy Barlow as a tiny man related to the dwarfs which McCullers used in her slightly earlier *Reflections in a Golden Eye* and *The Ballad of the Sad Cafe*, but he has nothing in common with Anacleto or Cousin Lymon, except diminished physical stature. Certainly he would refuse ever to allow himself to be seen as freakish or childlike.

"Madame Zilensky and the King of Finland" (1941), along with "The Jockey" and "The Sojourner" (1951), best exemplifies McCullers' ability to combine humor and pathos in the portrayal of characters who are likable but whose weaknesses make them vulnerable and who provide her with subjects for a mildly satirical art. In this story McCullers uses only two characters, both music professors at a small college, Mr. Brook and Madame Zilensky; and she explores with both delicacy and a sardonic mockery the relationship which develops between them. The rather colorless Brook, described as "a somewhat pastel" figure, has spent his life with Mozart minuets and "explanations about diminished sevenths and minor triads" (93). Madame Zilensky, his colleague-to-be, arrives from Europe with her three little boys to take over her new post, and a far from placid existence results for him as he gradually discovers that she embodies many of his own repressed impulses and aspirations. If Brook lectures quietly on musical theory, composition, and Mozart, the more inspired and imaginative Madame Zilensky teaches with dramatic force and fitful energy. Soon after her arrival, she finds four pianos for her studio and loses no time in setting "four dazed students to playing Bach fugues together. The racket that came from her end of the department was extraordinary" (95).

McCullers develops a complex pattern of contrasts between Brook and Madame Zilensky, and from these contrasts the organization of the story emerges. Harmony, as well as dissonance, characterizes their friendship. Mr. Brook's appreciation for "counterpoint" in musical composition relates metaphorically to his secret enjoyment of Madame Zilensky's departures from conventionality, logic, and quiet routine into a more zestful and creative world so different from his own conventional one. One also gradually recognizes that, while Brook and Madame Zilensky contrast with each other, each also possesses in his own right a kind of divided spirit, living a life that others see but also another life—secret, imaginative, and satisfying—which others are blind to or else see only intermittently. Mr. Brook can understand Madame Zilensky only because he himself lives a double life and achieves self-realization only in his fantasy world.

Madame Zilensky puzzles, exasperates, and fascinates Mr. Brook by the paradoxical nature of her personality and interests. She works to the point of exhaustion on what Brook considers her twelve "immense and beautiful" symphonies, but the next morning she remarks to him about the delightful evening she spent at a card party. His eyes light up a little when he listens to her oblique references to her adventures, world travels, lovers, and famous friends. She believes the fantasies that she reports—if only for the moment. For example, though all of her little boys look alike, she tells Brook one day about the father of each, all the time "thinking hard." Boris's father, she invents with a dreamy smile, was a Pole who played a piccolo. The father of Sammy, with whom she enjoys less rapport, was "that French," she declares indignantly, the man who probably still possesses her lost metronome. The absence of her metronome is the first thing that she mentions as she arrives on the train without her luggage in the opening of the story; and at various times, she becomes suddenly agitated about its disappearance, although she never replaces it. Curiously, Mr. Brook twice offers to give her his, but he never does; nor does she seem eager to acquire it. The metronome seems to symbolize the orderliness and conventionality lacking in her life of varying rhythms and imaginative elaborations. Her little boys also move to a rhythm of their own, as if in imitation of the idiosyncrasy of their mother. When they enter a room, they never step on the rug but carefully tiptoe around the edge of the room to keep their shoes on the floor.

Mr. Brook, on the other hand, is much more conventional and is more timid about giving actuality to his fantasies than is Madame Zilensky. He follows the rules of society and the regulations of his college, and he lives a life which is conscientious, orderly, and dull. But gradually his other life in the world of his imagination becomes dominant, and it draws him into Madame Zilensky's orbit and permits him to understand her—at least when he sits dozing by the fireside with a copy of Blake's poems and a glass of apricot brandy beside him and Mahler phrases drifting across his mind. Like Madame Zilensky, he is also a secret romantic and a psychic adventurer. When the music department had decided to "gang together"

for a summer in Salzburg, Brook vanished and went alone to Peru—
a gesture of self-assertion on his part and a rejection of the conventional expectations his colleagues have of him. In his brandied dreams, when his imagination soars, he identifies with Madame Zilensky's urge to invent the lies which "doubled the little of her existence that was left over from work" (99) and allow her to expand the self to its greatest possible dimensions.

Since Brook is, however, the revolutionary in theory who does not have the courage of his revolutionary predispositions, one day he wakes up, brushes his teeth, polishes his spectacles, and decides to assert the orderly side of his life and by implication feels it necessary to curb the imaginative excesses of his colleague. He now sees it as his duty to confront "the pathological liar." The pain, which he sees etched in her face when he accuses her of lying, so alarms him that he immediately begins encouraging her to continue her fable about the king of Finland, a country which has no king. "And was he nice?" Brook asks.

The intricate elaboration of the contrasts within each of the two characters, the contrasts established between the two people, and the similarity of their desire to transcend a dull reality contribute to the involuted and convoluted comic effects generated in this story. These effects are subtle and inhere as much in the unobtrusive behavior and basic tolerance of Mr. Brook as in the zestful and flamboyant eccentricity of Madame Zilensky. The intricacy of McCullers' technique in the story and the depth of the psychological exploration to be found in it are suggested by her use of contrapuntal patterns through which parallel characters and situations develop simultaneously, as it were, and reflect implicitly upon one another; by the vital presence of the music of Mahler, Mozart, and Bach; and also by the metronome as a symbolic illumination of the characters' tightly regulated lives. This story is McCullers' most thoughtful comedy, although "The Sojourner" is not far behind.

With much less depth of characterization and fullness of organization, McCullers in "Art and Mr. Mahoney" (1949) again makes music the background for the action and the characters' development. Using her keen sense for detail in phrase and manners, she satirizes the snobbery of music lovers at a concert and a reception. They display this snobbery toward Mr. Mahoney when he disgraces himself and his wife by clapping too soon and too enthusiastically at a pause in the program. All avert their eyes, his wife sits rigid and tense through the rest of the concert, and because of her humiliation, she converses with no one at the reception. Mahoney decides finally that he had a right to clap at what he enjoyed. Although the sketch makes its point as a satire upon ceremonious manners, its chief interest lies in its exposing the pretenses of provincially minded, so-called promoters of culture.

III *"A Tree, a Rock, a Cloud"*

After McCullers finished *The Ballad of the Sad Cafe,* she returned to Georgia late in 1941, to resume her difficult effort in balancing the "poetic and prosaic strands" in *The Bride,* which later became *The Member of the Wedding.* She had filed for divorce and was suffering severe psychic stress concerning her lost ability to pray and even to sign her name. At home in the South she was able to recover something of her shattered equilibrium. According to Virginia Spencer Carr, Carson gradually thought of her retreat to the quieter life of the South as comparable to Annemarie Clarac-Schwarzenbach's sojourn in Africa. Annemarie wrote her from there about the spiritual awakening she was experiencing in her primitive surroundings.

McCullers was intermittently writing poems during these years, and one of the outstanding short poems produced at this time was "The Twisted Trinity":

> There was a time when stone was stone
> When a face on the street was a finished face
> And a leaf, my soul, and God alone
> Made instant symmetry.
> Now all things fail, the trinity is twisted.
> Stone is not stone. And faces like the fractioned characters
> In dreams are incomplete.
> Until in the child's unfinished face I recognize
> Your sudden eyes.
> The soldier climbs the evening stair leaving
> Your shadow.
> And to the delicate autumn hill and the slant star
> The exiled intellect must add a new dimension:
> Something of you.[2]

In October, Klaus Mann published "The Twisted Trinity" in *Decision;* in December, David Diamond produced a musical setting for it; and Annemarie wrote that she had translated it into German and that it had so inspired her that she attempted to write a similar poem.

In "The Twisted Trinity" the speaker avers that formerly her life had been spiritually integrated, and she had then perceived a clear relationship among self, nature, and God—an "instant symmetry." Now a new presence—that of a lover—has not only disturbed this harmony, but has deepened it, in providing a new dimension and mystery to experience. No longer is stone only stone, nor a face a "finished face," but stone and face acquire an infinitude of significance which they had never before possessed. Though a later version of this poem, published as "Stone Is Not Stone" (1947), is less positive and suggests the adverse effects of the lover's absence, it retains the central idea that love has changed the total perception of the speaker.

When she finally recovered from a two-month battle with pneumonia in late January 1942, Carson attempted to express in fiction the main theme of "The Twisted Trinity": for any individual, love transforms the perception of the self, nature, and God. But as her allegorical story "A Tree, a Rock, a Cloud" took shape, she created instead a tale based on the inversion of two of the concepts that inform the poem. If in the poem the lover's presence suggests the significance and mystery in the simple things that surround the poet, in the story it is the beloved's desertion that makes the man frantic, driving him at first to search for her and later to discover salvation through the "science of love," which he has worked out in order to achieve a kind of spiritual therapy for his great grief. If in the poem, it is love which elicits the transcendent aspects of nature, in the story, McCullers reverses cause and effect, so that it is the close identification with nature which enables the protagonist once again to attempt love and to gain insight thereby into the transcendent aspects of sexual experience. By learning to love one small object or living thing at a time, the man hopes that he will eventually develop fully the ability to love a woman again, at least to love with greater understanding than he had been able to do previously.

McCullers builds her story around a tramp's progressive experience as he tries to put into practice his ideas concerning his newly formulated "science of love." As he sips his beer at dawn in an all-night cafe, barely managing to keep his big nose from dipping into the mug, he reminisces to a newsboy, whom he has forced to listen to his tale.[3] The protagonist searched for two years to recover the wife who deserted him before he discovered his "science," which requires that he try to experience feeling for a pet or an inanimate object, no matter how repulsive, and then turn toward the expression of feeling for human beings. He started with a goldfish, progressed to a stone, and now has travelled spiritually far enough to tell the child that he loves him. Actually, however, after he tells his tale, he shuffles away from the child without further thought of him; and the child simply shrugs, with some embarrassment, and comments to Leo, the cynical bartender, "He sure has done a lot of traveling" (139). The encounter provides no indication that the tramp has learned to love, to see the need for commitment to another person, or to inspire love.

Though McCullers often employed metaphor and used allegorical characters and situations in her longer fiction, this story stands alone among her short stories in its use of abstract figures and its focus on a fable with a directly stated philosophical message. Because the emphasis of the story is intellectual and abstract, the two main characters are deliberately left without names. They exist metaphorically simply as "the boy" and as "the man" or "the tramp." In certain other respects, however, the story illustrates some dominating characteristics of nearly all her short fiction, with its focus on only two or three characters, its brevity, its confinement to one problem or theme, its short time period, and its setting in one small room. Although some critics have praised it highly—even, in fact, regarding it as her best story—it remains, for me, too static to be among her finest narratives. Most importantly, perhaps, McCullers' attempt to convert a poem into a story represents from the first her versatility in experimentation with a variety of genres and patterns. The illumination this story gives to "The Twisted Trinity" and "Stone Is Not Stone" reflects her refusal ever to recognize a rigid demarcation between poetry and fiction. It also relates clearly to her effort at this time to attain in *The Bride* an intricate interweaving and balance of the poetic and prosaic.

IV   *The Elusiveness of Marital or Family Security*

McCullers in nearly all of her short stories, as in her long works, places her central characters within family groups. Most often, the family establishes a stable or permanent background against which the crisis affecting the single character is developed. In certain other works, however, like "The Haunted Boy," an individual's crisis derives directly from the family's crisis.

Three of the short stories reflect the situation of the family plagued by alcoholism: "The Instant of the Hour After," which preceded the marriage of Carson and Reeves McCullers, although it seems almost prophetic of their troubled relationship; "Who Has Seen the Wind?" (1956), in which alcoholism appears to be both cause and effect of the protagonist's "writer's block"; and "A Domestic Dilemma" (1951), in which the alcoholic is a young housewife and mother, who is distressed by the move from her small Southern town to a New York suburb, where she is isolated with small children.

"The Instant of the Hour After" is an exposé of the futility involved in the shiftless lives of alcoholics. After a guest leaves, the husband and wife argue derisively and interminably. The wife, who has recently decreased her own heavy drinking, has had during the evening a nightmarish glimpse of herself and her husband caught in a bottle, trying to climb up the glass wall, and failing. By the end of the evening, she feels contempt for her husband's arrogance and his insults directed toward the guest and herself, but she also feels anxiety and pity for him as he sits shaking with chills.

"Who Has Seen the Wind?" presents a similar couple and situation, although it is developed in several scenes—one revealing the alcoholic Ken's inability to continue his work as a fiction writer, another showing his contentiousness and insecurity in social situations, and still another, a crucial scene in which he shows his antagonism toward Marian, his wife, who has stopped drinking the previous year in alarm at the increasing violence of their quarrels. In this scene he is angered at her refusal to drink with him, and almost stabs and rapes her, but finally he lacks energy to express his hostility with overt violence and does not notice when she slips away. In a kind of postlude, the next day Ken wanders in the blinding snowdrifts toward certain suicide. The story reflects McCullers' lack of sure conception and organization in this rewritten version of a draft originally intended for the play *The Square Root of Wonderful*. Like the torment of the abusive and suicidal Phillip Lovejoy in that play, Ken's situation probably also reflects that of Reeves McCullers and, to some extent, that of Carson herself as a writer whose drinking seemed necessary to sustain her human relationships and even her writing, but which also interfered with them.

The first of these stories is an undeveloped sketch and the second, except for the violence of the final scene, is relatively monotonous in pace and disorganized; but both stories parallel, in the growing intensity of the woman's despair and in the mingled anger and compassion displayed for the alcoholic, the much more effective artistry of "A Domestic Dilemma" (1951). In this story McCullers attains greater depth in characterizing the individual caught between love and hate for a drunken spouse than in the other two tales, partly because Martin's characterization does not depend on a late-night harangue between two tired people, confused by alcohol. He arrives home from work, anxious about his children's safety, as he has been every day since Emily the year before dropped their baby on her head because she was too drunk to hold her. Martin's interaction is primarily with the children as he bathes and feeds them while his wife sleeps; the ambivalence of his feelings toward Emily gradually appears to the reader, though it is not evident to himself until the final moment of the story. As he bathes the children, he feels anger toward Emily for her inability to care for them and protect them, but as he feels tenderness for them when he bathes their bodies and when he watches them sleep, he finds waves of affection for Emily sweeping over him. When he is finally alone, fatigue, despair, and loathing for his wife overwhelm him. But again, as he prepares for bed, he looks at Emily, as he had gazed at the children in their sleep, and he is inexplicably drawn to her. Like the couple caught in the bottle in "The Instant of the Hour After," Martin sees himself and Emily caught together in bonds of suffering that are stronger than those of love, but those of love still survive. He slides into bed and reaches over, in his extreme weariness, simply to touch "the adjacent flesh," and life, for a moment, achieves again a glimmer of its lost radiance.

This story represents considerably greater artistry than that in either "The Instant of the Hour After" or "Who Has Seen the Wind?" particularly in its depiction of Martin's complex relationship with the other individuals—the children and Emily. The emphasis is only initially on Emily's drunkenness. The story also gains by McCullers' having extended her focus from Martin and his problems to those of Emily, though she appears directly in the story only for a few moments. She also suffers from the disharmony of the family situation. Her isolation, her homesickness for the South, and the guilt, anger, and love which she feels toward her children make her a considerable character, who finds a destructive release for unbearable tensions in her bouts of drinking. An irony exists in Martin's moments of great tenderness for his wife, experienced intermittently with his loathing for what she has become. It is as if he finds himself surprised that his love still exists and that there is still some urgency in his cherishing of her, since the bond between them has become so fragile. McCullers by this time in her career had gone beyond her early formulaic and quotable declarations in her fiction concerning the nature of love, deeply felt as they must sometimes have been. Love in this tale is a dominant and incomprehensible force, too complex to be separated from hatred, pity, memory, hope, or despair.

Like Martin in "A Domestic Dilemma," Ferris in "The Sojourner," another excellent story published only a few months earlier, reveals a man who is surprised by the strength of love and by his vulnerability with respect to it. Returning to Paris from his father's funeral in Atlanta, Ferris glimpses his former wife, Elizabeth, on the street in New York. Later, frustrated that he can reach no old friends by telephone, he impulsively calls her. That night as he briefly visits her home, she graciously serves him a surprise birthday cake, with thirty-eight candles, while he marvels that she looks like a Madonna with her children. He feels a tinge of jealousy for Elizabeth's new husband, a touch of anxiety about having lost his own youthful days, and a momentary grief—not just for his father's death but for the loss of his own family ties, which he had recognized in Atlanta the previous day and which he experiences again, and with greater intensity, with Elizabeth. He has been a sojourner—from the South, to New York, to Europe—and he has stopped only briefly in his journey for a few years of marriage. Mourning a death and celebrating a birthday so close together now ironically emphasize for Ferris the brevity of life, and he realizes he may be throwing away the best part of his own by being unable to commit himself to another person. The apparently idyllic life of Elizabeth's new family and the closeness of the family which he tried for a few days to rejoin in the South suggest to him that a sojourner who seeks the fullness of life by refusing to give up any of his freedom may, in actuality, miss the fullness of life. Back in Paris, he sits in the apartment of his sweetheart, Jeannine, waiting for her to return from the club where she sings and cuddling her lonely little son, whom he has previously tended to ignore.

But Ferris's new attempt to love is not at all selfless. He presses the child close in desperation as he feels "the terror, the acknowledgment of wasted years and death" and hopes that "an emotion as protean as his love could dominate the pulse of time"

(114). Ferris remains the type of the twentieth-century intellectual who is hedonistic, self-centered, and unable to learn from experience. One concludes that Ferris as sojourner may settle down to a committed love for Jeannine and Valentin, but that the roots he puts down may not be deep. He is so consistently treated with a touch of the satiric and the sardonic that one suspects that he will, in some sense, remain a sojourner in spite of the insights which his pilgrimage to his past has symbolically provided for him. Unfortunately, he may remain a person who accepts the momentary pleasure and the frustration of a man who is supposedly free but is in reality a hollow individual—a sojourner in this life, who evades its challenges and difficulties and so never achieves its rewards.

McCullers' interest in experimenting with various styles and genres was again manifested as she adapted this story as a successful play for television. It appeared on the "Omnibus" series as "The Invisible Wall" on December 27, 1953.

V *Poems*

Apart from "The Twisted Trinity" (1941) all of McCullers' published poems appeared in the late 1940s and early 1950s, immediately after she had persevered so long and succeeded so well in attempting to blend poetry and prose in *The Member of the Wedding*. Even "The Twisted Trinity" was revised during this period and reprinted as "Stone Is Not Stone." This was the time in her career when she enjoyed her greatest acclaim, with the Broadway success of *The Member of the Wedding* and the publication of the omnibus volume in 1951, but it was also a time of great psychic and physical stress. Physicians were raising her hopes and then disappointing her with various explanations for her strokes and predictions about her chances to regain some physical agility and to lessen her constant pain. Her second marriage to Reeves and their ever-growing dependence on alcohol increased her suffering until the distress culminated in his suicide in 1953.

In 1950 and 1951 she composed her most ambitious work of poetry, a cycle of five poems, "The Dual Angel: A Meditation on Origin and Choice." Some of these poems she wrote while she was being entertained by famous writers—Elizabeth Bowen at the ancient Bowen's Court near Dublin in 1950, Dame Edith Sitwell in England in 1951, and Princess Marguerite Caetoni, editor of

Botteghe Oscure, at her eleventh-century castle outside Rome in 1952. The cycle of poems, dedicated to Dame Edith Sitwell, appeared in 1952 in both *Botteghe Oscure* and *Mademoiselle.*

The five poems which comprise "The Dual Angel: A Meditation on Origin and Choice" range from ten to forty-seven lines: "Incantation to Lucifer," "Hymen, O Hymen," "Love and the Rind of Time," "The Dual Angel," and "Father, Upon Thy Image We Are Spanned." McCullers in the cycle explores the same apparently irresoluble conflict in Christian theology that had inspired Milton to compose *Paradise Lost:* "Why would an omnipotent God create mortals who are prone to sin?" A few of the lines, particularly in the "Incantation to Lucifer," possess some hint of the spiritual and aesthetic strength that Milton exhibited in *Paradise Lost* and reveal her command both of rhythm and imagery:

> Angel disarmed, lay down your cunning, finally tell
> The currents, stops and altitudes between Heaven and Hell.
> Or were the scalding stars too loud for your celestial velleities,
> The everlasting zones of emptiness uncanny to your imperious hand?
> (MH, 288)

She fails to sustain the heightened imaginative thrust that would have given the cycle of poems a consistent epical quality, not because of any lack of control of prosody or skill in versification, but because she attempts to use the same technique of alternating the formal with the colloquial in diction and phrasing, which she had so successfully mastered in a different medium, the short narrative. The heightened philosophical poem demands more unity and consistency than her kind of fiction did, so that the shifts from the philosophical to the mundane, from the tragic to the comic, seem incongruous in her poems, whereas in her prose, the yoking of such discordant elements often resulted in variety and a poignant irony. In the poetry the shifts appear as a lapse into the prosaic and destroy the unity of the poem, rather than creating an ironic effect. For example, in the opening poem of the long cycle she moves abruptly, after a few lines of formal incantation with lofty reference to "celestial velleities" or the angel's "imperious hand," to metaphors related to the commonplace in popular culture: "vulgar as a marathon dance," "neon lights," and "top-secret density." The alternation of colloquialisms with diction consistent with epic power is deliberate, not accidental, but her intent miscarries in the poems.

McCullers attains no valid fusion of the two modes of discourse that would betoken a viable aesthetic or philosophical unity.

Nevertheless, she is responsive to the worldly and the demonic, as well as to the godly, and apparently regards knowledge of the satanic as one means of achieving spiritual wisdom. Accordingly, she prefers Lucifer to Gabriel and calls upon him to relay to her the truth about his loss of paradise and its implications for mankind. Lucifer, however, gets no chance to speak; rather, the poet continues in a monologue in the "Incantation to Lucifer," to question, to speculate, and to fantasize about his fall from grace. In "Hymen, O Hymen," her personal myth of the creation of man centers on the marriage night of God and Lucifer, in which mankind was conceived. Belief in such a means for mankind's creation signifies that mankind need encounter no fall from purity and God's grace, since the human being has had from the beginning the capacity for evil as well as for good, for sin as well as for virtue, for the godlike and for the satanic. How and why God chose Lucifer that "cosmic night" remains a mystery that McCullers never quite fully elucidates. Perhaps God in furthering the reaches of cosmic love may have deliberately chosen as mate the individual furthest from the celestial beauty and virtue that He himself represents. For mortals, the hymeneal celebration in realms beyond the stars, and its reverberating consequences, can only be symbolized by "the protean firelight fearful on the wall," as emblematic in itself of God's spiritual power, as a love that overcomes all resistance including the demonic:

> There was no witness of this bridal night
> Only a zoic seascape and interlocking angels' might.
> So now we speculate with filial wonder,
> Fabricate that night of love and ponder
> On the quietude of Satan in our Father's arms:
> Velocity stilled, the restful shade.
> Satan we can understand—but what was God's will
> That cosmic night before we were made? (MH, 290)

Satan becomes the protagonist and an individual of heroic stature in the first three poems of the cycle. He strides from the rim of the ocean, across the shore, with "radiant grace and arrogance." As he moves with amazing velocity into the orbit of the earth, his "visage black with wind and sun," he feels the mysterious seas begin to move awesomely with the first life, as a result of the embraces that he experienced with God.

The audaciousness characterizing "Hymen, O Hymen" McCullers also sustains in the beginning of "Love and the Rind of Time." She rephrases, "What is man that Thou art mindful of him?" with an almost sacrilegious challenge implying that, after all, man is as important as God and that the rest of creation exists for him. She asks, "What is Time that man should be so mindful?" and proceeds to move, somewhat facetiously, through several lines in which she expresses diffidence about eons, ages, centuries, or millions and billions of years—all expressed in figures ordinarily expected to impress the human mind and possibly to strike fear and awe in the heart, but for her, figures impossible to conceptualize and, therefore, meaningless. Nevertheless, she suddenly declares, in one of the abrupt transitions characteristic of her poetry, the psalmist's own sense of the overwhelming insignificance of the mortal being in the presence of God and His creation. She suggests that she even feels a kind of terror at the realization that the life of all mankind on earth has been a mere "flicker of eternity," that under the aspect of eternity the human race may be of no greater significance than the primal cell, the "essential yeast":

> What is Time that man should be so mindful:
> The earth is aged 500 thousand millions of years,
> Allowing some hundred thousand millions of margin for error
> And man evolving a mere half-million years of consciousness,
>   twilight, and terror
> Only a flicker of eternity divides us from unknowing beast
> And how far are we from the fern, the rose, essential yeast? (MH, 290)

If McCullers in this cycle of poems considers such vast questions as the myths of creation, the battles waged on universal scale between mighty opposing forces, the millions of years of human history, and the moral complexities involved in the opposition between free choice and fate, she finally views in this third poem, "Love and the Rind of Time," such cosmic issues in light of the question that preoccupies her in many of her works of fiction—the beauty of love, the individual's need for it, his difficulty in attaining it, its inevitable fragility, and its awesome strength. McCullers hopes that a spiritual evolution, parallel to that in nature over billions of years, will allow mankind in future eons to understand the workings of love as the elemental resource that will inaugurate a true millennium at last:

> From weed to dinosaur through the peripheries of stars
> From furtherest star imperiled on the rind of time,
> How long to the core of love in human mind? (MH, 291)

The metaphors in the fourth poem, "The Dual Angel," relate to contemporary military strategy rather than to warfare waged in distant realms many light-years ago. They center on nuclear holocaust and the possibility that other "heirs of Lucifer," like herself, may end the world and bring extinction to the human race. One recognizes that this work was composed shortly after the bombing of Hiroshima and Nagasaki. The possible imminence of atomic warfare looms large in it, and the descriptions of Nagasaki and Hiroshima project her horror at the destruction wrought by mankind: "The screams are heard by blasted ears within the radiation zone / And hanging eyes upon a cheek must see the charred and irridescent craze" (MH, 292). The catastrophic agony that she experiences in the ruins resulting from the war cause her to cry, "Almighty God!"—an ironic exclamation, certainly, if God is omnipotent and capable of averting such tragedy. She identifies with the dazed multitudes who had no inkling that nuclear weaponry was being developed and who find themselves celebrating a joyful victory, though they are aware—but only partly—that suffering and destruction constituted that victory.

McCullers sees this century as the one interval separated from all the rest of human history and destined to become the "century of decision." She closes with a tentative optimism. Man who is capable of "transfigured vision" may yet save the human race from "obscenest suicide," but only if he can find some way of preventing the wholesale death and destruction that he has recently experienced. Mankind can no longer be complacent and adopt a spectator's stance toward what has happened; he must, rather, commit himself to some active program of social amelioration. Human beings can no longer be like "country children spangle-eyed at county fairs," who in their naiveté enjoy the thrill of a trapeze performance without regard to the dangers that the acrobats daily experience. Man's "furious intellect," McCullers in this poem views as a destructive force, because it has, in developing the atomic bomb, exalted abstractions at the expense of kinship among human beings.

Abstract intellectualism or rationalism is satanic, not only because of the devastation of the bombed cities but also because it can "split man from man" as it has split the atom. A Christ-like spirit of love and a courage to search for the elusive radiance in the cold lead and steel of modern life are the qualities that can mitigate mankind's situation if he will but be responsive to them.

In the prayer which comprises the final poem in the cycle, "Father, Upon Thy Image We Are Spanned," McCullers again considers the wretched aspect of the mortal existence in face of such an evil as nuclear warfare and mankind's possible options.[4] She ends with the same muted hope as in the preceding poem; but it is a tentative hope indeed, considering the evils of which human beings are capable, the demonic propensities of the human psyche, and the thin line which separates evil from good. Despite the horrors endemic in atomic warfare, the individual's heart can still "blaze with Christ's vision." The almost irresoluble problem is to inform political activity with the spirituality of which mankind is at least intermittently capable. Good does not lie in the absence of evil, but in the "synthesis" of good and evil which only can be wrought by God.

Though "The Twisted Trinity," "Stone Is Not Stone," and "The Dual Angel: A Meditation on Origin and Choice" represent a considerable poetic achievement, most significant of McCullers' poems in its craftsmanship may be "The Mortgaged Heart." The single theme developed in it is the "mortgage" which the beloved still holds, even after death, upon the heart of the lover, and the positive effect upon the mourner of this continued and demanding presence of the dead lover. Because the mourner remains inspired by his closeness to the dead, he finds a sense of direction, a pattern for renewed living, a sharpened sensitivity to the beauty of the world about him, and an increased sense of obligation to work to satisfy its needs. Thus, in any genuine sense, mourning is not a negative state but leads toward life instead of away from it and, in fact, doubles one's sense of being fully alive. The survivor's joy in the apprehension of the beauty of the world is increased, because he sees it not only with his own eyes, but refracted also through the eyes of the dead person whom he had cherished. Therefore, he watches twice "the orchard blossoms in gray rain" and "the cold rose skies," and gains a deepened sense of their beauty and spiritual significance. He also finds that his sense of duty is intensified since he must now react doubly to all calls made upon him. Whether the dead know of the payment of this tribute, does not really matter. Joy and virtue accrue in the life of the survivor.

The poem is characterized by great precision and compression and sustains a single thought with tautness from line to line. The simple form parallels the development of the thought. The initial three lines acknowledge the power of the dead to exact payment of love from those who mourn. The final three lines, in an ironic balance, suggest that the dead person who holds the mortgage, who seemed so imperious and demanding in the initial lines, may actually know nothing of the debt and of its conscientious repayment. That powerful one may now be simply "the secluded ash, the humble bone" and no longer involved with personal relationships.

Within this frame of opening and closing triplets, McCullers in the central eight lines develops the mourner's experience of grief and his feeling of intensified closeness to the dead. The last line, "Do the dead know?" seems, at first, not to be part of a closely unified poem. For one thing, it breaks the metrical pattern both because it is only a half-line and because it is a question. The question of whether the dead individual is sentient, however, is irrelevant in a poem which focuses upon the mourner's psyche and his salvation by means of his thoughts of the absent beloved. After McCullers' own death, her sister, Margarita Smith, edited her uncollected works and fittingly chose to call her tribute to Carson *The Mortgaged Heart* when it appeared in 1971.

VI   *A Second Play:* The Square Root of Wonderful

In McCullers' second play, *The Square Root of Wonderful,* the truth of love lies neither in the heart of the lonely hunter, nor in the reflections in a grotesquely romantic golden eye, nor in the magically warming influence of a potent liquor from a backwoods still, nor in a mystical wedding. Rather, she now suggests that scientific thought may account for the mysteries of love, a concept that she once before tentatively explored in her story "A Tree, a Rock, a Cloud." In *The Square Root of Wonderful,* she also approaches love rationalistically. Accordingly, the protagonist, John, an architect whom Mollie Lovejoy has met by chance the week before the play begins, instructs her that the truth of love lies not in the world of magic, as she had assumed all her life, but in the realm of logic. Mollie, awaiting the release from the sanatorium of her alcoholic husband, Phillip, has recognized her love for John, but does not yet see that love results from the exercise of the free will rather than from a spell cast upon one by fate. In John's mathematical formula to explain human emotions, the square root of sin for him is humiliation; the square root of wonderful is love. In such mathematics, love and humiliation cancel out each other. So Mollie's humiliation in her marriage can yield, if she wills it, to a powerful love that will set her free. Love alone can cancel out the debilitating humiliation she has always previously experienced in a sexual relationship.

The comedy in the play resides in the contrast between Mollie's lingering view of love as a romantic spell and her reluctance to accept John's new logic. She recalls that at age fifteen she was crowned "Peach Queen," and that on that same day love had bewitched her. She kissed a stranger, Phillip Lovejoy, made love with him in a berry patch, and recognized that she must, as a consequence, set their wedding date. Still subject to this powerful, irrational force, she clings to Phillip, even after years of abuse and degradation. Only when Phillip becomes a successful writer and humiliates her more grossly—by accusing her of using clichés—does his spell over her finally weaken.

After his return to her, the two impulsively reunite. He identifies his need for her as love; she mistakes her pity for him as love. By morning, Mollie recalls the lesson that John had taught her and determines to reject Phillip. But he has forestalled her rejection of him by deliberately subtracting himself from the world when he drives his car into the lake and drowns. Molly does not mourn him but accepts his death as something inevitable and welcome. Not tragedy, but a new beginning for John and Mollie dominates the closing of the play as their love achieves fruition.

Unlike *The Member of the Wedding,* the characters in this play generally reveal little emotion and psychic complexity. Only Mollie reveals much depth and complication. She is a contradictory figure; she remains the naive Peach Queen, while she also becomes the bold, vulgar woman who picks up an attractive hitchhiker and jokes about coveting her neighbor's ass. She is, moreover, the maternal figure who worries about the ill effects that her adolescent son, Paris, may suffer from his rich diet. She attains considerable self-awareness, furthermore, when she recognizes her solitariness among her self-centered relatives now that she has become an adult but has no one else who is spiritually adult to talk to.

Some effective comedy arises from the stereotypical characterization of Phillip's mother and sister. Sister, a librarian who habitually whispers, once fell in love with a man who checked out a book with a call letter in Z, and now creates in fantasy a variety of lovers from every country in the world with whom she can sin zestfully. Phillip's mother is perhaps more sinister than comic as McCullers envisages her. The mother's eccentricities are destructive because of her wish to humiliate her children. The need to humiliate others becomes the square root of her existence as a human being. She is obsessed with pride in her son's genius and with shame over her daughter's spinsterhood but loves neither of her children. To hide Sister's need for glasses as a child, she attempted to whisper the letters to the little girl as the oculist tested her eyes.

In the preface to the published version of the play (one of many scripts produced between 1952 and 1957), McCullers perceived the risks that she had undertaken in attempting to write a tragicomedy. A theater audience, she acknowledged, has difficulty in adapting without confusion to alternating scenes of tragedy and comedy, whereas a reader of fiction can accommodate more flexibly to a demand for mixed emotional response. McCullers also admitted in her preface that novelists like to write for the theater in order to experience "the unaccustomed joy of participating creatively with others" (S, ix - x), that is, when the play is rehearsed and mounted. This creative interplay with another person characterized the relationship between McCullers and Arnold Saint Subber, who worked almost daily with her between 1954 and 1957. Their relationship was also filled with tension as McCullers both welcomed and resisted his support and comradeship. Tennessee Williams stood by in many rehearsals, as he had supported her in the preparation for her first play. Three experienced directors worked through repeated changes in scenes and dialogues. The actors, though loyal, became discouraged after the second director resigned. Unfortunately, the joy of artistic creation with others, which characterized the production of *The Member of the Wedding*, did not develop for McCullers in the production of this play, because of her apprehension before it opened and because of her disappointment at its failure. While it was her hope to recreate in it the circumstances of Reeves's suicide and to "recreate my mother—to remember her tranquil beauty and sense of joy in life," she found that the definition of the complex "death-life" theme was often seemingly beyond her powers (S, viii). Moderating her aim, she then embodied her material in narrative form the year before the play opened and published it as the story "Who Has Seen the Wind?" (the title she used for most of the discarded scripts of the play). In the story she focused only on the growing hostility of the married couple and the destruction of the alcoholic husband and had apparently abandoned the attempt to incorporate elements of the comic in the work and to portray her mother in the wife.

The play failed five weeks after its opening at the National Theatre on Broadway, October 1957. Reviews focusing on the inadequacy of the play and its presentation had appeared earlier that month during its three-night run in Princeton and its two weeks in Philadelphia. The possible reasons for the failure led to much speculation. Albert Marre, the first director, had to resign because of schedule conflicts, but he saw value in the play, and he later remarked that McCullers may have been ahead of her time in producing a "black comedy." He also suggested that replacing Anne Baxter with Carol Channing might have brought out more sharply the ironic and comic elements present in the character of Mollie Lovejoy.[5]

Harold Clurman's analysis of the failure is especially illuminating, because he had adapted *The Member of the Wedding* for the theater. He called *The Square Root of Wonderful* a "total dud," and blamed both the directors and the actors; but he also placed responsibility on the author herself. He blamed her, not because she failed to adapt her writing adequately to the practical demands of the stage, but because she too willingly accommodated herself to these demands. She should have resisted all pressures "to make her story straightforward so that it might appear logical to the prosaic mind." He observed that her whimsicality, the unmotivated yet effective shifts in mood, the startling changes in character arising from conflicts deep in the psyche—all characteristic of her previous work—were in abeyance in this play. He contended that she should have allowed her script to retain "the faults natural to its author's genius," instead of tidying it up for reasons extrinsic to the work itself.[6]

In any event, McCullers did not sustain in her play the comedy to the point that it provided strong dramatic contrast as the play shifted toward pathos and tragedy. In her attempt to maintain pace, she provided for no continuous, interweaving conversations, such as those found in *The Member of the Wedding*. Except for Mollie, the play lacks vital characterization. It lacks, more damagingly, an adequate synthesis of the comic and the tragic elements that had been so insistent in her original conception of the work.

CHAPTER 8

Perspectives

THE reading of Carson McCullers' work provides the reader with a dynamic intellectual, spiritual, and aesthetic experience. Her gifts are manifold, intense, and varied. For one thing, she is a masterful portrayer of character as she gives simultaneously the essence of each individual and his idiosyncratic particularities. Her range as a portrayer of character is wide. Her black men and women never become mere stereotypes moving in the background. Her adolescent figures remain memorable as she treats them with humorous tolerance and with sympathetic understanding in their awkwardness, frustration, bitterness, confusion, and feelings of isolation. If her ordinary characters are memorable, the oddities of some of the others arrest, amuse, or shock. Such personages function symbolically or metaphorically, as well as realistically. In the few years in which she created her first four novels, her first play, and her best short stories, McCullers built a diverse world and filled it with people possessing great energy and forcefulness.

Besides her characterization, her artistry lay, to a considerable degree, in the remarkable virtuosity of her language—her blending of the poetic with the prosaic, of the formal with the colloquial, of the mystical and metaphorical perspective with the details of life in an ordinary small Southern town or a sleepy army post. Her poignant treatment of the tragic as well as her irrepressible humor, her sympathy for an unlovable individual as well as her unabashed confrontation of the cruelty of the powerful and frustrated indicate the breadth, inclusiveness, and compassion to be found in her work.

A master of realistic narrative, she could move easily into the symbolic, allegorical, and philosophical dimensions of her art. Her exploitation of the grotesque for dramatic or comic effects or to emphasize the isolation of the human being led her beyond realism to an experimentation with the gothic mode. Her ongoing sense of

145

the evil to be found in human nature and in a regimented society found expression in fiction which has symbolic and allegorical implications as she analyzes the elemental realities confronting her characters. Her portrayal of the South is, therefore, never sentimentalized; it is a land rich in folklore and colorful superstition but a land where "a man's life may be worth no more than a load of hay." It is a region where servants like Portia, Berenice, and Verily have dignity and become fully portrayed human beings, but where racial hatred brings tragedy to other blacks like Willie Copeland, Honey Camden Brown, Grown Boy, or Sherman Pew. It is a region where white workers, as well as black, in textile mills become "lint heads" who refuse to follow radical union organizers and are dehumanized by monotonous work. It is also a beautiful region where children hide in the shade of an arbor and smell the heavy scuppernong grapes or where one moves down heavily wooded trails covered with golden autumn leaves. Her awareness of the "voices and foliage" of the South enlivens the background of all her longer fiction, but much of the intensity of the fiction derives from the sense of isolation and homelessness that the characters experience wherever they are.

Ultimately, the universality of music more pervasively informs metaphor and background in her work than does a sense of geographical region. As Frankie Addams feels sorrow and frustration when music is interrupted before the scale is finished or the theme played out, one who reads McCullers finds so impressive the genius of her early work and so impressive the courage and endurance demanded of her throughout most of her career that the attempt to summarize her total achievement always seems premature. The music was interrupted before it should have been.

One could hazard that the richly talented and diversely gifted McCullers, as we know her, might finally have become a genius of the stature of George Eliot or Jane Austen or Edith Wharton. This is not to say that McCullers reveals only promise in her work. Her achievement is substantial and undeniable, but as in the case of her Southern contemporary Flannery O'Connor, we are continually haunted by the sense of what might have been had she lived long enough to consolidate her powers and to mature even more richly her artistry and her insights into human nature.

Notes and References

Chapter One

1. Margarita G. Smith, ed. *The Mortgaged Heart* (Boston, 1971), p. 285.
2. "The Flowering Dream," *The Mortgaged Heart*, p. 279. (Originally appeared in *Esquire*, Dec. 1959, 262 - 64).
3. Margaret S. Sullivan, *Carson McCullers, 1917 - 1947: The Conversion of Experience.* Unpublished Ph.D. dissertation (Durham, 1966), pp. 37 - 38.
4. Virginia Spencer Carr, *The Lonely Hunter* (New York, 1976), pp. 349 - 50.
5. Sullivan, pp. 189 - 90.
6. Carr, p. 153. See also pp. 371 - 74 on reunion with Diamond a decade later.
7. "The Vision Shared," *The Mortgaged Heart*, p. 262. (Originally appeared in *Theatre Arts*, April 1950, 38 - 40.)
8. "The Flowering Dream," pp. 276 - 77.
9. *Ibid.*, p. 275.
10. Carr, p. 121.
11. "The Flowering Dream," p. 275.
12. *Ibid.*, p. 277.
13. "Loneliness . . . An American Malady," *The Mortgaged Heart*, p. 260. (Originally appeared in *This Week, New York Herald Tribune*, Dec. 19, 1949, 19.)
14. *Ibid.*, pp. 260 - 61.
15. "The Vision Shared," p. 264.
16. Jan. 6, 1950, p. 26.
17. "The Vision Shared," p. 265.
18. *Ibid.*, p. 264.
19. "The Russian Realists and Southern Literature," *The Mortgaged Heart*," p. 252. (Originally appeared in *Decision*, July 1941, 15 - 19.)
20. "Isak Dinesen: *Winter's Tales*," *New Republic*, June 7, 1943. Also "Isak Dinesen: In Praise of Radiance," *Saturday Review*, Mar. 16, 1963, pp. 29, 83. (Both reprinted in *The Mortgaged Heart*, pp. 266 - 73.)

Chapter Two

1. "Author's Outline of *The Mute*," *The Mortgaged Heart*, p. 124.

147

2. *Ibid.*, p. 129.
3. *New Republic*, 103 (Aug. 5, 1940), 195.
4. Durham, 1965, p. 162.

Chapter Three

1. Critical comment on *Reflections in a Golden Eye* did not appear until its publication as a book in early 1941. During 1941 reviews appeared in major publications: *New Yorker, Saturday Review, Accent, Atlantic, Nation, New Republic, Time, Yale Review, New York Times Book Review, New York Herald Tribune* "Books," *Times Literary Supplement* (London), and *Boston Transcript*. Most of the reviewers expressed disappointment that the book was unlike the first novel—in its grotesque and morbid materials, its unsympathetic characters, and its lack of realism. Rose Feld, *New York Herald Tribune* "Books" (Feb. 16, 1941), sec. 9, p. 8, however, anticipated later writers in deeming the design and concentration of the second novel superior to the first. This view has been more recently expressed by Dale Edmonds, *Carson McCullers* (Austin, 1969); Richard Cook, *Carson McCullers* (New York, 1975); Louis Auchincloss, *Pioneers and Caretakers* (Minneapolis, 1965); and Tennessee Williams, *Reflections in a Golden Eye* (New York, 1950), pp. vii - xvii. I agree with the views of these critics concerning the masterful compression and structural sophistication of this novel.

Several later writers also used *Reflections in a Golden Eye* in allegorical interpretations of McCullers' work, particularly her treatment of themes related to love, loneliness, and personal identity. Chester Eisinger, *Fiction of the Forties* (Chicago, 1963), notes that here, as elsewhere, McCullers' characters are not only isolated from others but from parts of themselves; the male and female elements in the personality of each cause unresolved schisms particularly. Irving Malin, *New American Gothic* (Carbondale, 1962), suggests that patterns common to much gothic fiction in America are seen in this novel: self-love (and its inverse, self-hate), frightening family problems, travel to escape, and the sense of being alienated from oneself. Nicholas Joost, "Was All for Naught?" *Fifty Years of the American Novel: A Christian Re-Appraisal*, ed. Arthur Gardiner (New York, 1951), argues that the book is not artistically compelling but in its gothic effects advances profound metaphysical meanings.

I can agree with these later writers who see tantalizing allegorical implications underlying the strangeness of the characters and their behavior and their entrapment within so small a universe. Other writers who have used this novel in illustrating their critical theories have, I think, lost sight of the eccentricity of the characters and the irony implicit in the bitterly humorous narration. The essential protestantism and the "spiritualization of loneliness" in this example of gothic fiction, upon which Ihab Hassan elaborates in *Radical Innocence* (Princeton, 1961), or the comparison of this book with Plato's *Phaedrus* in an overview of Platonic elements in

McCullers' themes related to love, which Frank Baldanza discusses in "Plato in Dixie," *Georgia Review* (Summer 1958), 151 - 67, have stimulated critical interest in McCullers' art. However, I find that McCullers' books vary so much from one another that one must be cautious in using them as a group in expounding a theoretical approach.

2. Dale Edmonds, *Carson McCullers* (Austin, 1969), p. 17. Ellen Moers, *Literary Women* (New York, 1976), p. 108, also refers to medieval art in describing this book as "a kind of dance of doom."

3. Page numbers in parentheses throughout this chapter refer to *Reflections in a Golden Eye* as reprinted in *The Ballad of the Sad Cafe: The Novels and Stories of Carson McCullers* (Boston, 1951).

4. Virginia Spencer Carr, *The Lonely Hunter* (New York, 1975), pp. 107 - 08. McCullers was accepted at Bread Loaf in 1940, partly on the basis of a version of this novel. The director, Theodore Morrison, required some urging by Louis Untermeyer to accept her. He disliked some violent and grotesque incidents and disbelieved her defense that they were "hilariously funny." Wallace Stegner, who taught fiction at Bread Loaf that year and who conferred with her as she revised the book, also had doubts about the effect of some of the sequences.

5. McCullers, "The Russian Realists and Southern Literature," *Decision*, II (July 1941), 15 - 19. Reprinted in *The Mortgaged Heart*, pp. 252 - 58.

6. Virginia Spencer Carr, *The Lonely Hunter* (New York, 1975), p. 39; Lawrence Graver, *Carson McCullers* (Minneapolis, 1969); Clifton Fadiman, *New Yorker*, Feb. 15, 1941, p. 75; Mark Schorer, "McCullers and Capote: Basic Patterns," *The Creative Present*, ed. Nona Balakian and C. Simmons (Garden City, N.Y.: 1963), p. 89.

7. Letter to Robert Linscott, used on dustjacket of *Reflections in a Golden Eye* and reprinted in Carr's *The Lonely Hunter* (New York, 1975), p. 110.

Chapter Four

1. "I Wish I Had Written *The Ballad of the Sad Cafe*," in *I Wish I Had Written That*, ed. Eugene J. Woods (New York, 1946), pp. 300 - 301.

2. Page numbers in parentheses in this chapter refer to *The Ballad of the Sad Cafe: The Novels and Stories of Carson McCullers* (Boston, 1951).

3. For further comment on the narrator as related to the mythic quality of the book, see Dawson F. Gaillard, "The Presence of the Narrator in Carson McCullers' *The Ballad of the Sad Cafe*," *Mississippi Quarterly*, 25 (Fall 1972), 419 - 27; and Albert Griffith, "Carson McCullers' Myth of the Sad Cafe," *Georgia Review*, 21 (Spring 1967), 46 - 56. Also related to the mythic quality of the book is emphasis on the ballad form in the interpretation of the novel, as in Joseph Millichap, "Carson McCullers' Literary Ballad," *Georgia Review*, 27 (Fall 1973), 329 - 39. The need for interpretation of this work in terms of its characteristics as a lyrical ballad with mythic

implications may account for the negative reactions to Edward Albee's stage play based on the book. Cousin Lymon, in particular, could not be transferred to the stage without losing the sense of mystery and myth that surround him in the book.

Chapter Five

1. "The Vision Shared," *Theatre Arts*, April 1950, p. 30 (reprinted in *The Mortgaged Heart, p. 265*).

2. Marguerite Young's "Metaphysical Fiction" *(Kenyon Review*, 9 [Winter 1947], 151 - 55) is an early recognition of the novel as a philosophical one, rather than only as a tracing of adolescent development.

3. Reports on the war in Frankie's comments about the liberation of Paris suggest the book is laid in summer 1944. The play, in which Frankie speaks of the atomic bomb, is specifically laid in August 1945, the month that two bombs devastated Japanese cities.

4. Numbers in parentheses in this chapter refer to pages in *The Member of the Wedding* as reprinted in *The Ballad of the Sad Cafe: The Novels and Stories of Carson McCullers* (Boston, 1951).

5. Leslie Fiedler suggests this novel is a "homosexual romance" between Berenice and Frankie *(An End to Innocence: Essays on Culture and Politics* [Boston, 1955], p. 202). Frankie's immaturity and sexual naiveté, as well as Berenice's strong heterosexual interests, would argue against the plausibility of such interpretation.

Chapter Six

1. This book is dedicated to Dr. Mary Mercer, M.D., the psychiatrist and personal friend, who first met McCullers when she was experiencing depressive illness in 1958 and who remained her close companion until her death.

2. "Search for Identity: A Critical Survey of Significant Belles-Lettres By and About Negroes Published in 1961," *Phylon*, 23 (Summer 1962), 128 - 38.

3. "The World Outside," *New York Reporter*, September 28, 1961, p. 50.

4. "A Southern Drama," *Atlantic*, October 1961, pp. 126 - 27.

5. "The Author," *Saturday Review*, September 23, 1961, p. 15.

6. Robert O. Bowen, *New Catholic World*, 194 (December 1961), 186; and Henrietta Buckmaster, "The Break-Through and the Pattern," *Christian Science Monitor*, September 21, 1961. Buckmaster notes that the book attempts "to make assorted sickness attractive and real" and depicts "spiritually feckless people." However, she also states, "The writing is artful, and there are some beguiling scenes."

7. Page numbers in parentheses throughout this chapter refer to *Clock*

Without Hands (Boston, 1961). This novel is currently the only one by McCullers not in print.

Chapter Seven

1. In this chapter, page numbers in parentheses refer to *The Ballad of the Sad Cafe: The Novels and Stories of Carson McCullers* (Boston, 1951) unless they are preceded by *MH*, in which case they refer to *The Mortgaged Heart* (Boston, 1971), or *S*, in which case they refer to *The Square Root of Wonderful* (Boston, 1958).

2. *Decision*, II (Nov.-Dec. 1941), 30.

3. Both Oliver Evans in *The Ballad of Carson McCullers* and Virginia Spencer Carr in *The Lonely Hunter* suggest a parallel to Coleridge's *The Rime of the Ancient Mariner*, in the Mariner's insisting that the Wedding Guest hear the tale of his being forced to learn to love the insignificant creature.

4. Margaret Sullivan notes the similarity in the title and last line to a line in Rainer Maria Rilke's "Liebeslied": "Auf welches Instrument sind wir gespannt" (*The Poetry of Rainer Maria Rilke* [New York, 1938], p. 152). The love poem does not otherwise resemble McCullers' prayer. McCullers, like Annemarie Clarac-Schwarzenbach, loved Rilke's work, but she did not read German. She did, however, know long operatic arias in German and, at one time, hoped to learn German in order to translate Annemarie's work. McCullers once commented that the two poets she most enjoyed were Emily Dickinson and Hart Crane.

5. Carr, p. 453.

6. *Nation*, Nov. 23, 1957, p. 394.

Selected Bibliography

PRIMARY SOURCES

1. Collected Works
The Ballad of the Sad Cafe and Other Works. Boston: Houghton Mifflin, 1951. Contains, besides the title work, the other three early novels (*The Heart Is a Lonely Hunter, Reflections in a Golden Eye,* and *The Member of the Wedding*) and six stories ("Wunderkind," "The Jockey," "Madame Zilensky and the King of Finland," "The Sojourner," "A Domestic Dilemma," and "A Tree, a Rock, a Cloud").
The Mortgaged Heart, ed. Margarita G. Smith. Boston: Houghton Mifflin, 1971. Includes fourteen short stories, fifteen essays, and five poems, some not previously published.

2. Fiction
The Ballad of the Sad Cafe and Collected Short Stories. Boston: Houghton Mifflin, 1952. Contains the same short stories as *The Ballad of the Sad Cafe and Other Works* (1951), but not the three other novels. Second Edition (1955) adds "The Haunted Boy." *The Ballad of the Sad Cafe* originally appeared in *Harpers Bazaar,* August 1943, pp. 72 - 75, 140 - 61.
Clock Without Hands. Boston: Houghton Mifflin, 1961.
The Heart Is a Lonely Hunter. Boston: Houghton Mifflin, 1940.
The Member of the Wedding. Boston: Houghton Mifflin, 1946.
Reflections in a Golden Eye. Boston: Houghton Mifflin, 1941.

3. Plays
The Member of the Wedding. New York: New Directions, 1951.
The Square Root of Wonderful. Boston: Houghton Mifflin, 1958.

4. Children's Verse
Sweet as a Pickle and Clean as a Pig. Boston: Houghton Mifflin, 1964.

5. Short Stories
"Art and Mr. Mahoney," *Mademoiselle,* Feb. 1949, pp. 120, 184 - 86.
"Correspondence," *New Yorker,* Feb. 7, 1942, pp. 30 - 39.
"A Domestic Dilemma," *New York Post Magazine Section,* Sept. 16, 1951, p. 10.
"The Haunted Boy," *Botteghe Oscure,* 1955, pp. 264 - 78; and *Mademoiselle,* Nov. 1955, pp. 134 - 35; 152 - 59.
"The Jockey," *New Yorker,* Aug. 23, 1941, pp. 15 - 16.

"Madame Zilensky and the King of Finland," *New Yorker*, Dec. 20, 1941, pp. 15 - 18.

"The March," *Redbook*, Mar. 1967, pp. 69, 114 - 23.

"Mick," *Literary Cavalcade*, Feb. 1957, pp. 16 - 22, 32.

"The Pestle," *Mademoiselle*, July 1953, pp. 144 - 45 (later a part of *Clock Without Hands*).

"The Sojourner," *Mademoiselle*, May 1950, pp. 90, 160 - 66.

"Sucker," *Saturday Evening Post*, Sept. 28, 1963, pp. 69 - 71.

"To Bear the Truth Alone," *Harpers Bazaar*, July 1961, pp. 42 - 43, 93 - 99 (later a part of *Clock Without Hands*).

"A Tree, a Rock, a Cloud," *Harpers Bazaar*, Nov. 1942, p. 50.

"Who Has Seen the Wind?" *Mademoiselle*, Sept. 1956, pp. 156 - 57, 174 - 88.

"Wunderkind," *Story*, Dec. 1936, pp. 61 - 73.

6. Poems

"The Dual Angel," *Mademoiselle*, July 1952, p. 54; and *Botteghe Oscure*, 1952, pp. 213 - 18.

"The Mortgaged Heart," *New Directions*, 10 (1948), 509.

"Stone Is Not Stone," *Mademoiselle*, July 1957, p. 43.

"Sweet as a Pickle and Clean as a Pig," *Redbook*, Dec. 1964, pp. 49 - 56.

"The Twisted Trinity," *Decision*, 4 (Nov.-Dec. 1941), 30.

"When We Are Lost," *Voices*, 149 (Dec. 1952), 12.

7. Essays (Arranged Chronologically)

"Look Homeward, Americans," *Vogue*, Dec. 1940, pp. 74 - 75.

"We Carried Our Banners—We Were Pacifists Too," *Vogue*, July 15, 1940, pp. 42 - 43.

"Books I Remember," *Harpers Bazaar*, April 1941, pp. 82, 122, 125.

"Brooklyn Is My Neighborhood," *Vogue*, March 1941, pp. 62 - 63, 138.

"The Russian Realists and Southern Literature," *Decision*, 2 (July 1941), pp. 15 - 19.

"Isak Dinesen, *Winter's Tales*," *New Republic*, June 7, 1943, pp. 768 - 69.

"Love's Not Time's Fool," *Mademoiselle*, April 1943, pp. 95, 166 - 68.

"Our Heads Are Bowed," *Mademoiselle*, Nov. 1945, pp. 131, 229.

"How I Began to Write," *Mademoiselle*, Sept. 1948, pp. 256 - 57.

"Home for Christmas," *Mademoiselle*, Dec. 1949, pp. 53, 129 - 32.

"Loneliness, an American Malady," *This Week, New York Herald Tribune*, Dec. 19, 1949, pp. 18 - 19.

"The Vision Shared," *Theatre Arts*, April 1950, pp. 28 - 30.

"The Discovery of Christmas," *Mademoiselle*, Dec. 1953, pp. 54 - 55, 118 - 20.

"Playwright Tells of Pangs," *Philadelphia Inquirer*, Oct. 13, 1957, pp. 1, 5.

"The Flowering Dream: Notes on Writing," *Esquire*, Dec. 1959, pp. 162 - 64.

"A Child's View of Christmas," *Redbook*, Dec. 1961, pp. 31 - 34, 99 - 100.

"Author's Note," *New York Times Book Review,* June 11, 1961, p. 4.
"A Note from the Author," *Saturday Evening Post,* Sept. 28, 1963, p. 69.
"The Dark Brilliance of Edward Albee," *Harpers Bazaar,* Jan. 1963, pp. 98 - 99.
"Isak Dinesen: In Praise of Radiance," *Saturday Review,* March 16, 1963, pp. 29, 83.
"A Hospital Christmas Eve," *McCall's,* Dec. 1967, pp. 96 - 97.

SECONDARY SOURCES

1. Bibliographies

DORSEY, JAMES E. "Carson McCullers and Flannery O'Connor: A Checklist of Graduate Research," *Bulletin of Bibliography,* 32 (Oct.-Dec. 1975), 162 - 64. Lists theses and dissertations completed before Feb. 1975. Not annotated.

KIERNAN, ROBERT F. *Carson McCullers and Katherine Anne Porter: A Reference Guide.* Boston: G. K. Hall, 1976, pp. 95 - 169; 185 - 94. Arranged by year; books and articles separated; brief annotations; author index.

PHILLIPS, ROBERT S. "Carson McCullers, 1956 - 64: A Selected Checklist," *Bulletin of Bibliography,* 24 (Sept.-Dec. 1964), 113 - 16. Updates and enlarges a checklist by Stanley Stewart which covered from 1940 - 56. Includes records and films.

2. Books

CARR, VIRGINIA SPENCER. *The Lonely Hunter.* New York: Doubleday, 1976. Detailed and carefully researched biography. Little criticism of McCullers' works.

COOK, RICHARD M. *Carson McCullers.* New York: Ungar, 1975. Summary and comment on each major work. Sees her sympathy and insight into hidden suffering as her greatest attainment.

EDMONDS, DALE. *Carson McCullers.* Southern Writers Series, No. 6. Austin: Steck-Vaughn Co., 1969. Brief biography and commentary on works (43 pages). Incisive and succinct introduction to McCullers's work and life.

EVANS, OLIVER. *The Ballad of Carson McCullers: A Biography.* New York: Coward-McCann, 1966. Biography combined with thoughtful commentary on works. Some details conflict with biographies by Carr and Sullivan.

GRAVER, LAWRENCE. *Carson McCullers* (UMPAW 84). Minneapolis: University of Minnesota Press, 1969. Biography and discussion of each major work.

MALIN, IRVING. *New American Gothic.* Carbondale: Southern Ilinois University Press, 1962. Thematic organization, discussing gothic characteristics in six novelists. Basic in these writers (Capote, Hawkes, Salinger, Purdy, O'Connor, and McCullers) is use of narcissism and family terror. Dream device produces in characters a confusion of chronology, self-identity, and sexual orientation.

SULLIVAN, MARGARET S. *Carson McCullers: The Conversion of Experience, 1917 - 1947.* Unpublished Ph.D. dissertation, Duke University, 1966. Excellent biography. Uses interviews and correspondence, as does the later Carr biography, but focuses upon the relationship of McCullers' experience to her fiction.

WIKBORG, ELEANOR. *Carson McCullers' The Member of the Wedding: Aspects of Structure and Style.* Published dissertation, University of Goteborg, Sweden, 1975. Exemplifies the variety of current interest in McCullers. A linguistic study exploring the novel's "high degree of organization" through tabulation of patterns in rhythm and sound.

3. Parts of Books

CLURMAN, HAROLD. *Lies Like Truth.* New York: Macmillian, 1958, pp. 62 - 64. As director of "The Member of the Wedding," Clurman and three actors sensed the "direction" the play should take and its "inward action."

EISINGER, CHESTER E. *Fiction of the Forties.* Chicago: University of Chicago Press, 1963, pp 243 - 58. Thinks McCullers not concerned with social and regional issues but used the Southern mill town as symbol or as cause of certain behavior of her characters.

GOSSET, LOUISE. *Violence in Recent Southern Fiction.* Durham: Duke University Press, 1965, pp. 159 - 77. McCullers' violence tends to be a temporary condition, unlike the more inexorable violence in O'Connor. Violence in children's behavior may be a normal and healthy step toward maturity, unlike violence in her adult characters. Violence is overtly expressed, rather than repressed in the psyche.

SCHORER, MARK. "MCCULLERS AND CAPOTE: BASIC PATTERNS," *The World We Imagine.* New York: Farrar, Straus, and Giroux, 1968, pp. 274 - 96. Studies her lyrical and mythical transcendence of the social realities with which the books are apparently concerned, especially in *The Ballad of the Sad Cafe.*

4. Articles

BALDANZA, FRANK. "Plato in Dixie," *Georgia Review,* 12 (Summer 1958), 151 - 67. McCullers exalts Platonic love over Eros, but all love brings suffering. Sees McCullers as more closely related to Welty, O'Connor, and Capote than to Faulkner. Thinks her resemblances to Capote are pervasive.

FOLK, BARBARA. "The Sad Sweet Music of Carson McCullers," *Georgia Review,* 16 (Spring 1962), 202 - 209. Analysis of McCullers' use of music in the fiction: "always intelligent, functional, and openly reverent."

GAILLARD, DAWSON. "The Presence of the Narrator in Carson McCullers' *The Ballad of the Sad Cafe,*" *Mississippi Quarterly,* 25 (Fall 1972),

419 - 27. "The narrator's presence. . .lifts the story beyond the commonplace facts, beyond the immediate, and beyond history." His perspective yields a sense of "mythic proportion" to the work. Changes the town and a cafe from a place to a "state of mind."

GRIFFITH, ALBERT. "Carson McCullers' Myth of the Sad Cafe," *Georgia Review*, 21 (Spring 1967), 45 - 56. Lyricism overcomes perverse elements to make *The Ballad of the Sad Cafe* numinous and mystic rather than gothic or naturalistic.

HART, JANE. "Carson McCullers, Pilgrim of Loneliness," *Georgia Review*, 11 (Spring 1957), 53 - 58. McCullers differs from Eudora Welty and Truman Capote in her refusal to exploit abnormalities of characters for sensational effect.

HASSAN, IHAB. "Carson McCullers: The Alchemy of Love and Aesthetics of Pain," *Modern Fiction Studies*, 5 (Winter 1959), 311 - 26. Gothicism in McCullers' work is not sensational but spiritual or transcendental; her art is essentially subjective and introverted. Characters retreat to "inner rooms" and intensify pain of loneliness by disdaining Eros.

PHILLIPS, ROBERT S. "Dinesen's 'Monkey' and McCullers' 'Ballad,' " *Studies in Short FIction*, 1 (Spring 1962), 184 - 90. Comparison of characters and situations in the two works demonstrates McCullers' indebtedness, but tone differs.

PRESLEY, DELMA. "Carson McCullers and the South," *Georgia Review*, 28 (Spring 1974), 19 - 32. Thinks early work best because she had not "abandoned the landscape of her agony." Unlike other Southern writers "in exile," McCullers did not recover the South in imagination but separated herself from it a few years after she left. South threatened McCullers as a place which could entrap her in dullness, partly because she did not have aristocratic heritage in South.

Index

157